MAYA UNLIMITED
FEATURES

Credits:

Content Developers: Shawn Dunn, Petre Gheorghian, Scyalla Magloir, Cory Mogk, Rob Ormond

Copy Editor: Erica Fyvie

Technical Editors: Lenni Rodrigues, David Haapalehto

Cover Design: Louis Fishauf

Cover Image: Petre Gheorghian, Leon Vymenets

Production Manager: Carla Sharkey

Product Manager: Danielle Lamothe

Indexing: Bob Gundu

DVD Production: Roark Andrade, Julio Lopez

A special thanks goes out to:

Duncan Brinsmead, Susan-Belle Ferguson, Deion Green, Alan Harris, Tristan Ikuta, Rachael Jackson, Robert MacGregor, Vivien May, Cathy McGinnis, Danny Mousses, Jill Ramsay, Jason Schleifer, Michael Stamler, Larysa Struk, Alex Tang, Marcus Tateishi.

How to use this book

Learning Maya 6 | Maya Unlimited Features is your key to unlocking the power of Maya Unlimited Software. Learn to master Maya Fluid Effects, Maya Cloth, Maya Fur, and the powerful, new Maya Hair feature. This book is designed to help you comprehend Maya Unlimited regardless of your current skill level.

However, before you start this book, you should already have some knowledge of working in Maya as only those features available exclusively in Maya Unlimited are discussed in this book. For a broader understanding of the full Maya feature-set, you may want to explore *Learning Maya 6 | Foundation*.

Theoretical discussions

Each section of this book is introduced by a theoretical discussion explaining the concepts at play when working with various features. These sections will help you understand why and how Maya works so that you are better equipped to solve problems as your skills improve.

Project-based tutorials

Each chapter includes step-by-step tutorials to help you improve your skills when working with tools and features in Maya. Complete the full project for a broader understanding of the workflows or focus on specific tools to understand how they work.

Instructor overviews

View the Instructor overviews provided on the DVD-ROM for additional discussions and demonstrations to compliment the lessons in the book. Instructor overviews are provided by Alias Certified Instructors and are intended to act as your virtual trainer.

Index

Expert users may want to skip to the index in order find quick answers and solutions to production challenges without working through every lesson.

Updates to this book

In an effort to ensure your continued success through the lessons in this book, please visit our web site for the latest updates available:

www.alias.com/maya/learningtools_updates/

Installing tutorial files

In order to complete the lessons taught throughout the book, you will need to work in the Maya Unlimited 6 Software package. To install the tutorial scene files, copy the *support_files* directory from the DVD-ROM found at the back of this book onto your local hard drive.

Maya Unlimited Features

TABLE OF CONTENTS

CONTENTS

1 Maya Fluid Effects

Fluids are substances that change shape continuously or flow in response to forces. Maya® Fluid Effects™ is a new technology based on a branch of physics that employs mathematical equations (Navier-Stokes) to realistically simulate fluid motion. Using Fluid Effects, you can create a wide variety of 2D and 3D atmospheric effects (such as clouds or mist), pyrotechnic effects (such as explosions, smoke, and fire), space, and viscous liquid effects (such as molten lava). The Ocean shader was designed for creating realistic open water effects. You can float objects on the ocean surface and have those objects react to the motion of the water and generate wakes. In this chapter you will learn:

- How to create realistic atmospheric effects, such as clouds, and environment fog;

- How to create pyrotechnic effects, such as smoke, fire, explosions or nuclear blasts;

- How to affect geometry, cloth, and particles with fluids;

- How to use fluids as textures;

- How to create realistic open water effects with the Ocean shader and floating objects with foam and wakes.

Clouds

Fluids classification

In Maya, there are three basic types of fluid effects:

Dynamic fluid effects - behave according to the natural laws of fluid dynamics and simulate the effects by solving fluid dynamics equations for each time step. You can texture dynamic fluids, have them collide with and move geometry, affect soft body geometry or cloth objects, and interact with particles.

Non-dynamic fluid effects - use textures and animation to simulate fluid and fluid motion. These types of effects do not use fluid dynamics equations. You can create fluid motion by animating (keyframing) texture attributes. Because Maya doesn't solve the equations, rendering this type of fluid is much quicker than rendering a dynamic fluid.

Open water fluid effects - use shaders to create realistic wave motion on large bodies of water. Fluid containers can be used in combination with the Ocean shader to create wake and foam effects on the water.

Note: Dynamic and non-dynamic effects render as 3D volumes, so they interact appropriately with objects that move through them. In Maya, fluids can also be rendered with mental ray.

About fluid containers

The fluid container is the basis for any dynamic or non-dynamic fluid effect.

Note: Oceans do not require a fluid container, although they can interact with containers.

A fluid container is in fact a rectangular 2D or 3D boundary that defines the space in which the fluid can exist. Without boundaries, a dynamic fluid could conceivably deform into an infinite space (think of a dispersed gas) and your scenes would take forever to render. When you create fluid containers you can create them as either 2D or 3D containers. A 2D fluid container is really a 3D fluid container with a depth of one voxel. The size of that voxel is determined by the Z size of the container.

The benefit of using a 2D container is the considerably shorter rendering time, so in situations where you do not have geometry traveling through the container (e.g. an airplane flying through clouds), it is recommended to use a 2D container versus a full-fledged 3D fluid. Due to the extra data necessary to define them, 3D containers could be quite large, thus resulting in a very slow solve for the fluid dynamic behavior.

Note: Fluid containers can be placed within each other, but their contents will not interact with each other.

Contents Method

The Contents Method defines how a fluid property is defined in the container, if at all. There are two basic methods to define a fluid property in a fluid container:

- As a **Preset Gradient**;
- As a **Grid**.

Defining a fluid property as a **Preset Gradient** will maintain that property constant over time, and it sets a ramp of values from 1 to 0 on the respective axis.

Defining a fluid property as a **Grid** allows you to place individual values in each grid unit called a voxel (volume pixel), thus giving you more precise control over that property.

Grids could be defined as Static or Dynamic. **Static Grids** are used when you don't want the fluid property values to change over time (the values can be used in a dynamic simulation but they remain static over time).

Dynamic Grids are used to simulate dynamic behavior where the values in each voxel are being recalculated at each step using the fluid dynamic solver.

In many cases, you will combine static properties with dynamic properties to achieve a certain fluid effect (e.g. clouds moving in one direction would have a constant velocity acting upon a dynamic density).

Fluid states

The state of a fluid is a collection of its grid property values (the values in the Density, Velocity, Temperature, Fuel, Color, and Texture Coordinate grids). The state of an uncached dynamic fluid in any frame other than the first is based on its state in the prior frame.

Note: You have to cache a fluid simulation in order to be able to scrub through the timeline.

Initial State

The initial state represents the grid property values defined in a fluid container at the first frame of a simulation. When you play a simulation up to any frame, you can use the current state at that frame as the initial state.

If, for example, you have an empty fluid container but you want to start the simulation with fluid already in it, you could add an emitter to the container, play and stop the simulation at the frame containing the desired amount of fluid, and then set the emitted fluid values as the initial state.

To set the Initial State:
- Select the fluid container.
- In the **Fluid Effects** menu, select **Set Initial State**.

Modifying the behavior and contents of a fluid

By modifying the attributes of the fluid container you change the appearance and behavior of the fluid. For example, if you change the Gravity value (found under the Dynamic Simulation section of the Attribute Editor for the fluid container) to a negative value, the Density will fall instead of rise.

Note: No matter what changes you make to the attributes, the fluid can never leave the container. A fluid can only exist inside a container.

You can also edit the contents of a fluid container using the **Paint Fluids Tool** found under **Fluid Effects → Add/Edit Contents**.

To paint contents into a container:
- With the container still selected, choose **Fluid Effects → Add/Edit Contents → Paint Fluids Tool - ❑**.

  The Tool Settings window opens and a slice displays at the origin of the fluid container. The slice is represented by a plane with dotted edges and fluid subvolume manipulators at one corner. When you move the pointer over the slice the pointer changes to a brush indicating that you can paint.
- At the top of the Tool Settings window, click **Reset Tool** to set the **Paint Fluids Tool** Settings to the default values.
- Select the fluid properties you want to paint in the **Paint Attributes** section of the Tool Settings window.

  You could paint each property separately, but in some cases it is more efficient to paint two of them at the same time.

Tip:	You can display numeric values for Density, Temperature, or Fuel in the grid by changing the Numeric Display in the **Display** section of the fluid Attribute Editor. This way you can visualize the values as you paint.

Container size and resolution

Over the course of the following exercises, we will look at several combinations of methods that will help us achieve the desired result. There are situations when you will want to modify the size of the fluid container. Scaling the container will change the size of the voxels but not their content; thus the fluid content will look thinner. Changing the container size in the Attribute Editor for the *fluidShape* node changes the size of the voxels including the voxel content, scaling everything proportionally.

If you need finer detail for your fluid simulation, you will have to increase the resolution.

The size should be proportional to the resolution to get consistent quality on all axes. For example, if the container size is 10, 5, 2 then a valid resolution would be 20, 10, 4. If the size is not proportional to the resolution, the quality will be higher along one axis than on another axis.

To increase the Fluid Resolution:

- Select the fluid container.
- In the **Dynamics** menu set, select **Fluid Effects** → **Edit Fluid Resolution - ◻**.
- Enter the desired number of voxels and click **Apply and Close**.

Be aware that increasing the fluid resolution will considerably increase the rendering time due to the larger number of voxels that need to be evaluated by the fluid solver.

ATMOSPHERIC EFFECTS

Within the next exercise, we will take a look at how we can combine fluid containers with a different Contents Method in order to achieve environment fog and cloud effects that can interact with the existing geometry.

Creating realistic clouds

In this exercise, you will create a relatively detailed cloud with rapidly evolving animation using 3D fluid containers. Within the exercise, the Density of the clouds fluid container will be defined as a constant gradient while the Opacity Input will be defined as a Y gradient and textured with Perlin Noise (which is the standard 3D noise used in the Solid Fractal texture), to control the details. The clouds will animate with a simple expression applied to the Texture Time attribute of the Perlin Noise.

Cloud effects with textured 3D fluids

1 Open CloudsMT_Start.mb

- From the *scenes* directory on the Support Files DVD-ROM, open the file named *CloudsMT_Start.mb*.

2 Create a 3D fluid Container

- Under the **Fluid Effects** menu, select **Create 3D Container**.

- In the Channel Box, rename the fluid to *Clouds*.

- Translate the container **3** units on the Y-axis.

- In the Channel Box, enter **3.0** for **Scale** on X, Y, and Z.

3 Adjust the Resolution and Size

- Select the 3D container and open the Attribute Editor.

- In the **Container Properties** section, enter the following values:

  Resolution to **60, 6, 60**;

  Size to **20, 2, 20**.

  Changing the resolution proportionally will maintain a uniform look for the rendered fluid.

4 Adjust the fluid contents

- In the Attribute Editor for the *Clouds* fluid, open the **Contents Method** section and set the following settings:

    Density to **Gradient**;

    Density Gradient to **Constant**;

    Velocity to **Off(zero)**;

    Temperature to **Off(zero)**;

    Fuel to **Off(zero)**;

    Color Method to **Use Shading Color**.

- Press **6** on your keyboard to see the fluid in hardware texturing mode.

5 Adjust the Shading of the Clouds fluid

- In the Attribute Editor for the *Clouds* fluid, open the **Shading** section and set the following settings:

    Dropoff Shape to **Y Gradient**.

    This will set a ramp of values between 1 and 0 for the density on the Y direction.

    Edge Dropoff to **0.372**.

    This defines the rate at which the **Density** values drop off.

    Click on the **Transparency** swatch and set the following HSV values:

    H to **205.0**;

    S to **0.000**;

    V to **0.778**.

6 Adjust the fluid Color

- Within the **Shading** section, open the **Color** sub-section, click on the color swatch for the **Selected Color** and set the following HSV values:

    H to **336.0**;

    S to **0.089**;

    V to **0.598**.

7 Adjust the fluid Incandescence

The Incandescence controls the amount and color of light emitted from regions of density due to self-illumination, and it is found in the **Shading** section under the **Incandescence** sub-section.

- Select the first color entry in the Incandescence ramp (by clicking the dot indicating the ramp marker), and enter the following value:

  Selected Position to **0.429**.

- Change the HSV values of the first color entry to:

  H to **238.0**;

  S to **0.300**;

  V to **0.279**.

- Select the second color entry in the Incandescence ramp and enter the following value:

  Selected Position to **0.550**.

- Change the HSV values of the second color entry to:

  H to **231.0**;

  S to **0.300**;

  V to **0.268**.

- Select the third color entry in the Incandescence ramp and enter the following value:

  Selected Position to **0.857**.

- Change the HSV values of the third color entry to:

  H to **231.0**;

  S to **0.547**;

  V to **0.301**.

- Set the **Incandescence Input** to **Y Gradient**.

8 Adjust the fluid Opacity

Opacity represents how much the fluid blocks light and it can be found in the **Opacity** sub-section of the **Shading** section.

- Set the **Opacity Input** to **Y Gradient**.
- Set the **Input Bias** to **0.1**.
- Change the **Selected Position** for the first entry in the Opacity graph to **0.5**.

- Click inside the Opacity graph to add a new entry and enter the following values:

    Selected Position to **0.507**;

    Selected Value to **0.360**.

- Click inside the Opacity graph to add a new entry and enter the following values:

    Selected Position to **0.586**;

    Selected Value to **0.660**.

- Click inside the Opacity graph to add another entry and enter the following values:

    Selected Position to **0.671**;

    Selected Value to **0.860**.

- The last entry in the Opacity graph should have the following values:

    Selected Position to **1.000**;

    Selected Value to **1.000**.

9 Assigning a Perlin Noise texture to the Opacity

- In the Attribute Editor for the *Clouds* fluid open the **Textures** section.
- Set **Texture Opacity** to **On**.
- From the **Texture Type** choose **Perlin Noise** (the standard 3D noise used in the Solid Fractal texture).
- Set the following values for the **Perlin Noise** attributes:

    Amplitude to **0.942**;

    Ratio to **0.620**;

    Frequency Ratio to **3.752**;

    Depth Max to **4**;

    Inflection to **On**;

    Frequency to **1.5**;

    Implode to **0.256**.

10 Create an expression to drive Texture Time

- In the **Texture Time** attribute text field, type the following expression:

    ```
    =time*0.5
    ```

- Press **Enter** on your keyboard to confirm the creation of the expression. This expression will reduce the speed of the animated texture to half of the current time value so the clouds will appear to move slower.

11 Adjust the Lighting for the Clouds fluid

- Open the **Lighting** section and choose the following settings:

  Self Shadow to **On**;

  Hardware Shadow to **On**;

  Real Lights to **On**.

12 Creating another 3D container for the Sky

- Under the **Fluid Effects** menu, select **Create 3D Container**.

- In the Channel Box, rename the fluid to *Sky*.

13 Adjust the Resolution and Size of the Sky fluid

- Select the 3D container and open the Attribute Editor.

- In the **Container Properties** section, enter the following values:

  Resolution to **20, 20, 20**

  Size to default **(10, 10, 10)**.

- In the Channel Box, change the **Scale** to **12, 6, 12**.

14 Adjust the fluid Contents

- In the Attribute Editor for the *Sky* fluid, open the **Contents Method** section and choose the following settings:

  Density to **Gradient**;

  Density Gradient to **Constant**;

  Velocity to **Off(zero)**;

  Temperature to **Off(zero)**;

  Fuel to **Off(zero)**;

  Color Method to **Use Shading Color**.

15 Adjust the Transparency of the Sky fluid

- In the Attribute Editor for the *Sky* fluid, open the **Shading** section and choose the following values for **Transparency**:

  H to **205.0**;

  S to **0.000**;

  V to **0.838**.

16 Adjust the Sky fluid Color

- Within the **Shading** section, open the **Color** sub-section, select the first color entry, and enter the following values:

  Selected Position to **0.371**;

  H to **194.0**;

  S to **0.484**;

  V to **0.160**.

- Click inside the ramp to create a new ramp entry and enter the following values:

  Selected Position to **1.000**;

  H to **190.0**;

  S to **0.315**;

  V to **0.612**.

- Set the **Color Input** to **Y Gradient**.

17 Texture the Opacity of the Sky fluid

- Open the **Textures** section and set **Texture Opacity** to **On**.

- Under **Texture Type** choose **Perlin Noise** and use the default values.

18 Render your scene

- Open the **Render Globals** window and choose mental ray from the **Render Using** drop down menu at the top (mental ray should be set to **On** in the Plugin Manager window).

- Under the mental ray tab of the Render Globals window, choose **Production** from the **Quality Presets** drop down menu.

- Choose the desired resolution and render the scene.

Note: In Maya, you can render your fluid containers with mental ray for Maya.

PYROTECHNIC EFFECTS

There are several ways to simulate pyrotechnic effects with fluid containers. During the following exercises, we will look at a few of these methods used to simulate smoke, fire and explosions. Some of the examples will use fluid containers with their contents set to Dynamic Grids while others will combine Dynamic Grids with Gradients and Textures to achieve the final result.

Creating smoke effects

In this exercise, we will use a 2D fluid container to simulate cigarette smoke. The density and velocity of the fluid will be dynamically evaluated and the motion will be driven by the Buoyancy and Swirl attributes. This type of fluid effect would be useful in scenes with limited camera movement where a quick smoke effect is required.

Smoke effect using a 2D fluid container

1 Open Ashtray_Start.mb

- From the *scenes* directory on the Support Files DVD-ROM, open the file named *Ashtray_Start.mb*.

2 Create a 2D fluid container with an emitter

- Under the **Fluid Effects** menu select **Create 2D Container with Emitter**.

- In the Channel Box, rename the fluid to *Smoke*.

- Translate the container to the following values:

    Translate X to **2.264**;

    Translate Y to **7.808**.

3 Adjust the Resolution and Size

- Select the 2D container and open the Attribute Editor.

- In the **Container Properties** section, enter the following values:

    Resolution to **80, 120**;

    Size to **10, 15, 0.250**.

4 Move the 2D fluid emitter

- In the Perspective view, select *fluidEmitter1* and using the **Move Tool**, move it on X and Y until it is inside the tip of the cigarette. Make sure that you don't move it on Z.

5 Adjust the 2D fluid emitter attributes

- In the Attribute Editor for *fluidEmitter1*, open the **Basic Emitter Attributes** section and set the **Max Distance** to **0.140**.

- Open the **Fluid Attributes** section and set the **Density/Voxel/Sec** to **3**.

6 Adjust the fluid Contents

- In the Attribute Editor for the *Smoke* fluid, open the **Contents Method** section and choose the following settings:

    Density to **Dynamic Grid**;

    Velocity to **Dynamic Grid**;

    Temperature to **Off(zero)**;

    Fuel to **Off(zero)**;

    Color Method to **Use Shading Color**.

- Press **6** on your keyboard to see the fluid in hardware texturing mode.

7 Adjust the fluid Gravity

- In the Attribute Editor for the *Smoke* fluid, open the **Dynamic Simulation** section and set **Gravity** to **20**.

8 Adjust the fluid Density and Buoyancy

If the Buoyancy value is positive, then the Density represents a substance that is lighter than the surrounding medium and will thus rise (negative values cause the Density to fall).

- In the Attribute Editor for the *Smoke* fluid, open the **Contents Details** section and then open the **Density** sub-section and set the following:

  Density Scale to **1**;

  Buoyancy to **12**;

  Dissipation to **0.700**;

  Diffusion to **0**.

9 Adjust the fluid Swirl

- In the Attribute Editor for the *Smoke* fluid, open the **Contents Details** section and then open the **Velocity** sub-section and set the following:

  Swirl to **8**.

10 Adjust the fluid Turbulence

- In the Attribute Editor for the *Smoke* fluid, open the **Contents Details** section and then open the **Turbulence** sub-section and set the following:

  Strength to **0.100**;

  Speed to **0.030**.

11 Adjust the fluid Transparency

- Within the **Shading** section, click on the color swatch for **Transparency** and set the following HSV values:

  H to **0.00**;

  S to **0.00**;

  V to **0.060**.

12 Adjust the fluid Opacity

Opacity represents how much the fluid blocks light and it can be found in the **Opacity** sub-section of the **Shading** section:

Set the **Input Bias** to **-0.121**.

13 Playback the simulation

- Set your playback end to **300** and playback the simulation.

Creating fire effects

In this exercise we will use a 3D fluid container that has the Contents Method set to Dynamic Grid, except for the Color Method. The motion of the flame is controlled by the Buoyancy, Swirl, Turbulence and Reaction Speed. The Incandescence, which controls the amount and color of light emitted from regions of Density, is driven by the Temperature. Opacity uses Density as an input and there is no texturing assigned. The Opacity ramp determines the shape of the flame, particularly the edges.

The Incandescence controls the color and the actual Color ramp is set to black. In this example, the Incandescence ramp uses "super white" entries (values greater than 1). The interpolation to black will produce intermediate orange and red colors similar to the color variation from flames of varying temperature.

Fire effect using a 3D fluid container

1 Open Fire_Start.mb

- From the *scenes* directory on the Support Files DVD-ROM, open the file named *Fire_Start.mb*.

2 Create a 3D fluid container with an emitter

- Under the **Fluid Effects** menu, select **Create 3D Container with Emitter**.

- In the Channel Box rename the fluid to *Fire*.

- Translate the container to the following values:

  Translate Y to **3.876**;

  Translate Z to **1.289**.

3 Adjust the Resolution and Size

- Select the 3D container and open the Attribute Editor.
- In the **Container Properties** section, enter the following values:

  Resolution to **30, 30, 30**;

  Size to **10, 10, 10**.

4 Move the 3D fluid emitter

- In the Perspective view, select *fluidEmitter1* and using the **Move Tool**, move it on the **Y-axis** until it is under the wood geometry.

5 Adjust the 3D fluid emitter attributes

- Open the **Fluid Attributes** section and set the following values:

  Density/Voxel/Sec to **1**;

  Heat/Voxel/Sec to **2**;

  Fuel/Voxel/Sec to **4**.

- Open the **Fluid Emission Turbulence** section and set the following:

  Turbulence to **1.157**.

6 Adjust the fluid Contents

- In the Attribute Editor for the *Fire* fluid, open the **Contents Method** section and choose the following settings:

  Density to **Dynamic Grid**;

  Velocity to **Dynamic Grid**;

  Temperature to **Dynamic Grid**;

  Fuel to **Dynamic Grid**;

  Color Method to **Use Shading Color**.

- Press **6** on your keyboard to see the fluid in hardware texturing mode.

7 Change the Simulation Rate Scale

The Simulation Rate Scale changes the time step used in emission and in solving.

- In the Attribute Editor for the *Fire* fluid, open the **Dynamic Simulation** section and set the following:

  Simulation Rate Scale to **2**.

8 Adjust the fluid Buoyancy

- In the Attribute Editor for the *Fire* fluid, open the **Contents Details** section, then open the **Density** sub-section and set the following:

  Buoyancy to **9**;

  Dissipation to **0.182**.

9 Adjust the fluid Swirl

- In the Attribute Editor for the *Fire* fluid, open the **Contents Details** section and then open the **Velocity** sub-section:

  Set **Swirl** to **10**.

10 Adjust the Turbulence Strength

- In the Attribute Editor, open the **Contents Details** section and then open the **Turbulence** sub-section:

  Set **Strength** to **0.010**.

11 Adjust the Temperature

- In the Attribute Editor, open the **Contents Details** section and then open the **Temperature** sub-section:

  Set **Temperature Scale** to **1.934**;

  Set **Buoyancy** to **9.000**.

12 Adjust the Fuel

- In the Attribute Editor for the *Fire* fluid, open the **Contents Details** section and then open the **Fuel** sub-section:

  Set **Fuel Scale** to **1.967**;

  Set **Reaction Speed** to **0.967**.

13 Adjust the Transparency of the Fire fluid

- In the Attribute Editor for the *Fire* fluid, open the **Shading** section and choose the following values for **Transparency**:

  H to **194**;

  S to **0.000**;

  V to **0.772**.

- Set the **Dropoff Shape** to **Sphere**.

- Set the **Edge Dropoff** to **0.446**.

14 Adjust the fluid Color

- Within the **Shading** section, open the **Color** sub-section and set the color to **black**.

15 Adjust the fluid Incandescence

The Incandescence controls the amount and color of light emitted from regions of Density due to self illumination, and it is found in the **Shading** section under the **Incandescence** sub-section.

- Select the first color entry in the Incandescence ramp (by clicking the dot indicating the ramp marker), and enter the following value:

    Selected Position to **0.657**.

- Change the HSV values of the first color entry to:

    H to **15.00**;

    S to **0.815**;

    V to **15.00**.

- Set the **Interpolation** to **Smooth** for the first color entry.

- Select the second color entry in the Incandescence ramp and enter the following value:

    Selected Position to **1.000**.

- Change the HSV values of the second color entry to:

    H to **15.00**;

    S to **0.815**;

    V to **0.000**.

- Set the **Incandescence Input** to **Temperature**.

- Set the **Input Bias** to **-0.297**.

16 Adjust the fluid Opacity

Opacity represents how much the fluid blocks light, and it can be found in the **Opacity** sub-section of the **Shading** section.

- Set the **Opacity Input** to **Density**.

- Set the **Input Bias** to **0.315**.

- Change the **Selected Position** for the first entry in the Opacity graph to **0.136** and set the **Selected Value** to **0.000**.

- Set the **Interpolation** to **Spline** for the first entry.

- Click inside the Opacity graph to add a new entry and enter the following values:

    Selected Position to **0.137**;

    Selected Value to **0.540**.

- Set the **Interpolation** to **Linear** for the second entry.

- Click inside the Opacity graph to add a new entry and enter the following values:

    Selected Position to **0.329**;

    Selected Value to **0.220**.

- Set the **Interpolation** to **Spline** for the third entry.

- The last entry in the Opacity graph should have the following values:

    Selected Position to **0.857**;

    Selected Value to **0.020**.

- Set the **Interpolation** to **Spline** for the last entry.

17 Adjust the Shading Quality

- Within the **Shading** section, open the **Shading Quality** sub-section and set the **Quality** to **5.000**.

    This setting will increase the number of samples per ray used to render, thereby increasing the quality of the render.

18 Playback your fluid simulation

Creating an explosion effect

In this exercise we will simulate a nuclear blast using a 3D fluid container. The animation happens due to the density buoyancy. The color of the fluid is based on its density. The texture applied enhances the details of the explosion cloud.

1 Open Nuke_Start.mb

- From the *scenes* directory on the Support Files DVD-ROM, open the file named *Nuke_Start.mb*.

2 Create a 3D fluid container with an emitter

- Under the **Fluid Effects** menu, select **Create 3D Container with Emitter**.

- In the Channel Box, rename the fluid to *Nuke*.

- Translate the container to the following value:

  Translate Y to **4.992**.

3 Adjust the Resolution and Boundaries

- Select the 3D container and open the Attribute Editor.
- In the **Container Properties** section, enter the following values:

  Resolution to **30, 30, 30**;

  Boundary Y to **-Y side**.

Note: The fluid doesn't actually leave the container where there are no boundaries, it just looks that way. Fluids can only exist inside a container.

---

4 Adjust the 3D fluid emitter attributes

- Select the fluid emitter and open the Attribute Editor.
- Open the **Transform Attributes** section and set the following values:

  Translate Y to **-4.383**;

  Scale X and **Scale Y** to **2.940**;

  Scale Z to **0.538**.

- Open the **Basic Emitter Attributes** section and set the **Emitter Type** to **Volume**.
- Open the **Emitter Attributes** section and set the following values:

  Density/Voxel/Sec to **2**;

  Fluid Dropoff to **5.992**.

- Open the **Volume Emitter Attributes** section and set the **Volume Shape** to **Sphere**.

5 Adjust the fluid Contents

- In the Attribute Editor for the *Nuke* fluid, open the **Contents Method** section and choose the following settings:

  Density to **Dynamic Grid**;

  Velocity to **Dynamic Grid**;

  Temperature to **Off(zero)**;

  Fuel to **Off(zero)**;

  Color Method to **Use Shading Color**.

- Press **6** on your keyboard to see the fluid in hardware texturing mode.

6 Adjust the fluid Density, Buoyancy, and Diffusion

- In the Attribute Editor for the *Nuke* fluid, open the **Contents Details** section and then open the **Density** sub-section and set the following:

    Density Scale to **1**;

    Buoyancy to **8**;

    Diffusion to **0.030**.

7 Adjust the fluid Swirl

- In the Attribute Editor for the *Nuke* fluid, open the **Contents Details** section and then open the **Velocity** sub-section:

    Set **Swirl** to **12**.

8 Adjust the fluid Turbulence Strength

- In the Attribute Editor, open the **Contents Details** section and then the **Turbulence** sub-section:

    Set **Strength** to **0.020**.

9 Adjust the Transparency of the fluid

- In the Attribute Editor for the *Nuke* fluid, open the **Shading** section and choose the following values for **Transparency**:

    H to **14.46**;

    S to **0.000**;

    V to **0.171**.

- Set the **Glow Intensity** to **0.194**.
- Set the **Dropoff Shape** to **Cube**.
- Set the **Edge Dropoff** to **0.233**.

10 Adjust the fluid Color

- Within the **Shading** section, open the **Color** sub-section, select the first color entry, and enter the following values:

    Selected Position to **0.143**.

- Click on the color swatch and set the color to **black**.

- Click inside the ramp to create a new ramp entry and enter the following values:

  Selected Position to **0.771**;

  H to **14.46**;

  S to **0.648**;

  V to **0.179**.

- Click inside the ramp to create another ramp entry and enter the following values:

  Selected Position to **0.857**;

  H to **11.86**;

  S to **0.974**;

  V to **1.269**;

  Color Input to **Density**.

- Click inside the ramp to create the last ramp entry and enter the following values:

  Selected Position to **1.000**;

  H to **14.46**;

  S to **0.916**;

  V to **6.000**;

  Color Input to **Density**.

- Go to frame **1** in the timeline and set the **Input Bias** to **0.848**.

- **RMB-click** on the **Input Bias** numeric input field and choose **Set Key**.

- Go to frame **54** in the timeline and set another keyframe for the **Input Bias** with the same value (**0.848**) by clicking with the **RMB** on the numeric input field and choosing **Set Key**.

- Go to frame **74** in the timeline and set another keyframe for the **Input Bias** with the same value (**0.848**) using the same method.

- Go to frame **200** in the timeline and change the value for the **Input Bias** to **564** and set another keyframe using the same method.

  Animating the Input Bias will affect the Color distribution and Glow Intensity during the simulation.

11 Adjust the fluid Incandescence

- Select the first color entry in the Incandescence ramp (by clicking the dot indicating the ramp marker), and enter the following value:

  Selected Position to **0.257.**

- Change the color of the first color entry to **black**.

- Select the second color entry in the Incandescence ramp and enter the following value:

  Selected Position to **0.336.**

- Change the HSV values of the second color entry to:

  H to **147.41**;

  S to **0.105**;

  V to **0.077**.

- Select the third color entry in the Incandescence ramp and enter the following value:

  Selected Position to **0.471.**

- Change the HSV values of the third color entry to:

  H to **51.14**;

  S to **0.484**;

  V to **0.153**.

- Click inside the Incandescence ramp to add a new entry and enter the following value:

  Selected Position to **0.564.**

- Change the color of the last entry to **black**.

- Set the **Incandescence Input** to **Center Gradient**.

- Set the **Input Bias** to **-0.022**.

12 Adjust the fluid Opacity

Opacity represents how much the fluid blocks light and it can be found in the **Opacity** sub-section of the **Shading** section. Set the following:

  Opacity Input to **Density**;

  Input Bias to **0.550**.

- Change the **Selected Position** for the first entry in the Opacity graph to **0.127** and set the **Selected Value** to **0.000**.

- Set the **Interpolation** to **Linear** for the first entry.

- Click inside the Opacity graph to add a new entry and enter the following values:

    Selected Position to **0.214**;

    Selected Value to **0.280**.

- Set the **Interpolation** to **Spline** for the second entry.
- Click inside the Opacity graph to add a new entry and enter the following values:

    Selected Position to **0.343**;

    Selected Value to **0.520**.

- Set the **Interpolation** to **Spline** for the third entry.
- Leave the last entry unchanged.

13 Assigning a texture to Color, Incandescence, and Opacity

- In the Attribute Editor for the *Nuke* fluid, open the **Textures** section.
- Set **Color, Incandescence** and **Opacity** to **On**.
- From the **Texture Type** choose **Space Time** (a 4-dimensional version of the Perlin Noise where time is the 4th dimension).
- Set the following values for the **Space Time** texture attributes:

    Color Tex Gain to **1.000**;

    Incand Tex Gain to **0.300**;

    Opacity Tex Gain to **0.800**;

    Amplitude to **2.300**;

    Ratio to **1.00**;

    Frequency Ratio to **3.000**;

    Depth Max to **2**;

    Inflection to **On**;

    Frequency to **1.00**.

14 Create an expression to drive the texture time

- In the **Texture Time** attribute text field, type the following expression:

    ```
    =time*0.8
    ```

- Press **Enter** on your keyboard to confirm the creation of the expression.

15 Playback the simulation

AFFECTING GEOMETRY WITH FLUIDS

With the force of a fluid you can move or modify geometry, move cloth objects, or particles. You can also collide the contents of a fluid container with geometry. Over the following exercises we will take a look at some of these options.

Colliding geometry with fluids

The following steps illustrate how to get the contents of a fluid container to collide with geometry.

1 Create a dynamic fluid container

- Under the **Fluid Effects** menu, select **Create 3D Container with Emitter**.

- Make sure that under the **Contents Method** section in the Attribute Editor, **Density** and **Velocity** are set to **Dynamic Grid**.

2 Move the geometry inside the fluid container

- Select the geometry and move it inside the fluid container.

3 Create the dynamic connection between the geometry and the fluid

- Select both the geometry and the fluid container (order is not important) and select **Fluid Effects** → **Make Collide**.

4 Playback the simulation

- Using the playback controls in the timeline, play your simulation

---

Note: For better quality results, increase the Tessellation on the *geoConnector* node (found under the Outputs for the geometry in the Channels Box).

Tip: Set the fluid Render Interpolator to linear if you notice the fluid passing through the geometry (found in the Shading Quality section of the Attribute Editor).

Using fluids to move geometry

In the next exercise you will use the force of a fluid to move geometry by making the geometry an Active Rigid Body.

1 **Create a 3D fluid container with an emitter**

- Under the **Fluid Effects** menu, select **Create 3D Container with Emitter**.

- Make sure that under the **Contents Method** section in the Attribute Editor, **Density** and **Velocity** are set to **Dynamic Grid**.

- Select the fluid emitter and move it close to the bottom of the container.

2 **Move the geometry inside the fluid container**

- Select the geometry that will be affected by the fluid force and move it inside the fluid container, above the emitter.

3 **Make the geometry an Active Rigid Body**

- Select the geometry and go to the **Soft/Rigid Bodies** menu and select **Create Active Rigid Body**.

4 **Adjust the rigid body Performance**

- Open the Attribute Editor for the *rigidBody* node and open the **Performance Attributes** section. Set the **Apply Force At** option to **centerOfMass** to ensure that the fluid affects the rigid body as expected.

5 **Make the connection between the fluid and the rigid body**

- Select both the fluid container and the geometry (order doesn't matter).

- Go to the **Fields** menu and choose **Affect Selected Object(s)**.

6 **Playback the simulation**

- Using the playback controls in the timeline, play your simulation.

Note: You can modify the look of the simulation by modifying both the fluid attributes or the rigid body, adding fields, etc.

Using fluids to modify geometry

This exercise will use the force of a fluid to change the shape of geometry by making the geometry into a soft body.

1 **Create a 3D fluid container with an emitter**

- Under the **Fluid Effects** menu, select **Create 3D Container with Emitter**.

- Make sure that under the **Contents Method** section in the Attribute Editor, **Density** and **Velocity** are set to **Dynamic Grid**.

2 **Move the geometry inside the fluid container**

- Select the geometry that will be affected by the fluid force and move it inside the fluid container, above the emitter.

- Make sure that the geometry has enough resolution to make the deformation obvious (e.g. for a NURBS plane increase the number of patches on U and V to 7).

3 **Make the geometry a soft body**

- Select the geometry and select **Soft/Rigid Bodies → Create Soft Body - ▢**.

- Under **Create Options**, choose **Duplicate, Make Copy Soft**.

- Set **Make Non-Soft a Goal** to **On**.

- Set the **Weight** to **0.1**.

4 **Make the dynamic connection**

- With both the copy of the geometry and the fluid container selected, go to the **Fields** menu and choose **Affect Selected Object(s)**.

5 **Playback the simulation**

- Using the playback controls in the timeline, play your simulation.

USING FLUIDS TO MOVE CLOTH

In the following exercise we will create a cloth object and then we will use the force of a fluid to it.

1 **Create a 3D fluid container with an emitter**

- Under the **Fluid Effects** menu, select **Create 3D Container with Emitter**.

- Make sure that under the **Contents Method** section in the Attribute Editor, **Density** and **Velocity** are set to **Dynamic Grid**.

2 **Create a cloth object**

- Create a NURBS plane and scale it until it just fits inside the fluid container, then place it above the fluid emitter.

- In the Channel Box, under the **Inputs** section, select *makeNurbPlane1* and change the number of patches on U and V to **8**.

- In the Cloth menu, select **Create Cloth Object**.

3 Make the connection between the cloth object and the fluid

- In the Perspective window select the fluid container, then **RMB-click** onto the cloth object, and choose vertex from the marking menu.

- **Shift-select** the vertices of the cloth object (the fluid container should still be selected).

- With both the fluid container and the cloth vertices selected, go in the **Constraints** menu (of the Cloth menu), and select **Field** to apply the fluid as a field to the cloth.

4 Lower the cloth Bend and Stretch Resistance

- Select the cloth object and in the Channel Box, under the **Inputs** section, select cpDefaultProperty.

- Lower the **U** and **V Bend Resistance** values to a value of **1**.

- Lower the **U** and **V Stretch Resistance** values to a value of **5**.

5 Change the Gravity

- With the cloth object selected in the Channel Box; under the **Inputs** section, select the *cpSolver* and change **Gravity** to **0**.

6 Playback the simulation

- Using the playback controls in the timeline, play your simulation.

Note: For any modification you make before you playback your simulation, go under the Simulation menu and select Delete Cache.

MOVING PARTICLES WITH FLUIDS

In the next section, we will take a look at how particles can be moved with the force of a fluid.

1 Create a 3D fluid container with an emitter

- Under the **Fluid Effects** menu, select **Create 3D Container with Emitter**.

- Make sure that under the **Contents Method** section in the Attribute Editor, **Density** and **Velocity** are set to **Dynamic Grid**.

2 Create a particle shape

- Select **Particles** → **Particle Tool** - ❑.

- Set the **Number of Particles** to **20**, **Maximum Radius** to **4** and **Conserve** to **0.2**, and sketch particles within the Perspective view.

3 Move the particle shape inside the container

- Select the particle shape and move it inside the fluid container. The particles must be inside the container to be affected by the fluid.

4 Make the dynamic connection between the particles and the fluid

- Select both the particle shape and the fluid and go into the **Fields** menu and choose **Affect Selected Object(s)**.

5 Playback the simulation

- Using the playback controls in the timeline, play your simulation.

USING FLUIDS AS TEXTURES

Fluids can be also used as texture maps for common shaders such as Lambert, Blinn, etc. This allows for generating very interesting effects that would be much more difficult to achieve otherwise. The next exercise will take you through an example of texturing geometry with a 3D fluid.

Using a 3D fluid to texture a logo

This exercise uses a 3D fluid container with both Density and Velocity contents set to Dynamic Grid. The Density content has the Viscosity and Friction attributes set to values different than zero for a more liquid look, and the Simulation Rate Scale is set to a value smaller than one. The animation of the fluid contents happens due to the Density and Buoyancy, and the Perlin Noise texture assigned to the Color, Incandescence and Opacity. The Perlin Noise has the Texture Time attribute mapped with a simple expression that reduces the speed in relationship with the current time. The Lambert shader assigned to the logo geometry has the Glow Intensity attribute set to a value higher than zero for the glowing effect.

1 Open FluidLogo_Start.mb

- From the *scenes* directory on the Support Files DVD-ROM, open the file named *FluidLogo_Start.mb*.

2 Assign the fluid texture to the logo shader

- Select **Window** → **Rendering Editors** → **Hypershade...**

- **MMB-drag** the logo shader from the **Materials** tab of the Hypershade into the Work Area (the bottom portion of the Hypershade).

- Click on the **Textures** tab of the Hypershade window and **MMB-drag** the *FluidTextureShape* node onto the logo shader icon found in the Work Area of the Hypershade.

- Choose **Color** from the pop-up menu. This will connect the *outColor* of the *FluidTextureShape* node to the color of the logo shader.

3 Playback your simulation

In order to see the effects of the fluid texture on the logo geometry, you will have to playback your simulation.

- Using the playback controls in the timeline, play your simulation.

4 Render your animation

- Select **Window** → **Rendering Editors** → **Render Globals...**

- Click on the **Common** tab, and set **Frame/Animation Ext** to **name.#.ext**.

- Set your **Start Frame** to **1** and the **End Frame** to **300**.

- Open the **Resolution** section and choose the resolution you desire.

- Go to the **Render** menu and select **Batch Render**.

CREATING OPEN WATER EFFECTS

With Fluid Effects, you can easily create a variety of realistic water surfaces, from high seas with foam to ponds or swimming pools. Although fluid containers are not necessary when creating oceans, both oceans and ponds can interact with them.

In Maya there are two ways to create open water effects:

- Creating oceans, which are defined by a flat surface with an Ocean shader assigned to it. Fluid Effects simplifies the process by providing a single command that creates a plane optimized for best results and an Ocean shader with the appropriate connections.

- Ponds are 2D fluids that use a spring mesh solver and a height field. With the pond options and attributes, you can set the size and color of your fluid surface. Ponds are good for creating swimming pools or smaller bodies of water.

Overview of oceans

The Ocean shader can be used to simulate a wide range of water wave patterns, from stormy sea swells to bathtub waves and it generates the waves through displacement. The shading of the ocean surface has been turned off for hardware playback (since it would slow down the playback considerably), and the only way to preview the animation is a *heightField* node used as a Preview Plane. This allows you to interactively adjust the look of the displaced waves without having to render the file. The Preview Plane can be scaled (only on the X and Z-axis since Y is controlled by the height of the displacement), and moved anywhere across the NURBS surface used by the Ocean shader. It will not appear in the rendered images. It can also be parented to an object floating on the ocean surface (e.g. it could be parented to a floating boat), thus allowing for previewing the animation of the waves for any floating object. The resolution of the Preview Plane can be adjusted if necessary (in the Attribute Editor for the *oceanPreviewPlane* node), but any substantial increase will result in a slower playback of the ocean simulation.

Fluid Effects also allow you to create floating objects such as regular boats or motor boats through the help of dynamic locators. They also provide a large number of parameters including throttle, rudder, and roll that allow for controlling the animation and appearance of the floating objects (found in the Extra Attributes section of the Attribute Editor for the dynamic locators). You could either animate the floating objects by using the above mentioned attributes for the dynamic locators or by keyframing the X and Z position of the locators over time (you will have to set the Free Transform option to On in the options box when you make the geometry into any type of floating object).

Over the course of the following exercises we will take a look at the attributes of the Ocean shader, learn what they represent and how they can be adjusted in order to achieve predictable results. We will also see how 3D fluid containers can be used in conjuction with the Ocean shader to create wake and foam effects for the floating objects.

Fluid Effects include a series of example files that are found in the Visor and include all the components and settings for different ocean effects. You can quickly import them into your file, modify them to customize the effects, or study them to better understand how to create your own oceans.

To create an ocean or pond using an example file:

- In the Dynamics menu set, select **Fluid Effects → Get Ocean/Pond Example**... The Visor window will open at the **Oceans** tab.

- **MMB-drag** the icon of the example you want into your scene. Maya will import all the objects that are part of that effect into your scene.

- Playback the simulation and adjust any objects or attributes to customize the effect.

Creating a stormy ocean

During the next exercise, we will explore the attributes of the Ocean shader node, their functionality, and how they can be adjusted to achieve a stormy deep sea effect. The Time attribute has been used to animate the water surface through a simple expression =time (created by default when you create an ocean). This generates approximate animation for an ocean Scale value of 1. A 3D fluid container with textured opacity has been used to generate the environment fog effect above the water surface.

Stormy ocean effect using the Ocean shader

1 Create the ocean surface

- In the Dynamics menu set, select **Fluid Effects** → **Ocean** → **Create Ocean** - ❏ and set:

    Create Preview Plane to **On**.

- Click on **Create Ocean**.

2 Adjust the Wind UV values

The Wind UV controls the direction that the waves will travel similar to the way wind does in real life. This is expressed as U and V values (in the UV texture space).

- Open the Attribute Editor for the *oceanShader1* node and then open the **Ocean Attributes** section.

- Set the **Wind UV** values to **0.800** and **0.300**.

3 Adjust the Wave Frequencies, Direction, and Length

- Open the Attribute Editor for the *oceanShader1* node and then open the **Ocean Attributes** section.

- Set the **Num Frequencies** to **6**.

  Num Frequencies controls the number of interpolated frequencies between Wave Length Min and Wave Length Max. The higher this value, the longer this texture will take to compute. If this value is not an integer, the number of created frequencies will be the rounded up value.

- Set the **Wave Dir Spread** to **0.200**.

  Wave Dir Spread defines the variance in wave direction with respect to the wind direction. If set to zero, then all waves travel in the same direction. If it is set to one, then the waves travel in random directions.

- Set the **Wave Length Min** to **0.100**.

  Wave Length Min controls the minimum length of waves in meters.

- Set the **Wave Length Max** to **45**.

  Wave Length Max controls the maximum length of waves in meters.

4 Adjust the Wave Height

The **Wave Height** controls the size of the waves relative to their wave length. The left edge of the graph represents waves with the shortest wave length and the right edge represents waves with the longest wave length. The values range between Wave Length Min and Wave Length Max.

- Select the first entry in the Wave Height graph and enter the following:

  Selected Position to **0.000**;

  Selected Value to **0.050**.

- Click inside the Wave Height graph to add a new entry and enter the following values:

  Selected Position to **0.150**;

  Selected Value to **0.100**.

- Click inside the Wave Height graph to add another entry and enter the following values:

  Selected Position to **0.640**;

  Selected Value to **0.160**.

- Click inside the Wave Height graph to add the last entry and enter the following values:

     Selected Position to **1.000**;

     Selected Value to **0.160**.

5 Adjust the Wave Turbulence

This attribute controls the amount of turbulence at different wave frequencies. The left edge of the graph represents waves with the shortest wave length and the right edge represents waves with the longest wave length. The values range between Wave Length Min and Wave Length Max. This is the most computation expansive attribute.

- Select the first entry in the Wave Turbulence graph and enter the following values:

     Selected Position to **0.000**;

     Selected Value to **1.000**.

With a value of one, the wave motion will be completely turbulent at different frequencies.

6 Adjust the Wave Peaking

This attribute controls the amount of crest formation for waves across the range of wave frequencies. The Wave Turbulence must be different than zero for this attribute to have an effect as it only applies to turbulent waves.

- Select the first entry in the Wave Peaking graph and enter the following values:

     Selected Position to **0.000**;

     Selected Value to **0.0280**.

- Click inside the Wave Peaking graph to add a new entry and enter the following values:

     Selected Position to **0.157**;

     Selected Value to **0.640**.

- Click inside the Wave Peaking graph to add another entry and enter the following values:

     Selected Position to **0.364**;

     Selected Value to **0.740**.

- Click inside the Wave Peaking graph to add the last entry and enter the following values:

  Selected Position to **1.000**;

  Selected Value to **0.560**.

7 Add foam to the waves

- Set the **Foam Emission** to **0.180**.

  This attribute controls the density of foam generated above the foam threshold

- Set the **Foam Threshold** to **0.615**.

  This attribute controls the Wave Amplitude required to generate foam and determine how long the foam will last.

- Set the **Bump Blur** to **0.500**.

  This attribute, when set to larger values, has the effect of making small waves and peaks look smoother.

8 Adjust the Common Material Attributes

- Open the Attribute Editor for the *oceanShader1* node and then open the **Common Material Attributes** section.

- Click inside the Water Color swatch and enter the following values:

  H to **182.59**;

  S to **0.761**;

  V to **0.835**.

- Set the **Refractive Index** to **1.350**.
- Set the **Diffuse** to **0.495**.
- Set the **Trough Shadowing** to **1.000**.

  This attribute makes the wave peaks look brighter and it darkens the wave troughs. It works well when the water has a blue-green color.

- Set the **Translucence** to **0.282**.
- Set the **Translucence Depth** to **20**.

9 Adjust the Specular Shading

- Open the Attribute Editor for the *oceanShader1* node and then open the **Specular Shading** section.
- Set **Specularity** to **0.447**.

- Set **Eccentricity** to **0.165**.
- Set **Reflectivity** to **0.971**.

10 Adjust the environment

- This attribute defines a simple sky to ground environmental reflection using a ramp. The left of the ramp represents the top of the sky while the right is the bottom.
- Select the first color entry in the Environment ramp (by clicking the dot indicating the ramp marker), and enter the following value:

    Selected Position to **0.08**.

- Change the color of the first ramp entry to **black**.
- Select the second color entry in the Environment ramp and enter the following value:

    Selected Position to **0.393**.

- Change the HSV values of the second color entry to:

    H to **192.87**;

    S to **0.578**;

    V to **0.026**.

- Select the third color entry in the Environment ramp and enter the following value:

    Selected Position to **0.570**.

- Change the HSV values of the third color entry to:

    H to **190.78**;

    S to **0.142**;

    V to **0.851**.

- Click inside the Environment ramp to add a new color entry and enter the following value:

    Selected Position to **0.750**.

- Change the HSV values of the fourth color entry to:

    H to **202.16**;

    S to **0.663**;

    V to **0.669**.

- Click inside the Environment ramp to add the last color entry and enter the following value:

    Selected Position to **1.000**.

- Change the HSV values of the last color entry to:

    H to **210.24**;

    S to **0.837**;

    V to **0.547**.

11 Create a 3D fluid container for the environment fog

- Using the techniques learned previously in the Atmospheric Effects section of this chapter create a 3D fluid container and adjust its contents to get an environment fog effect above the water surface.

Creating a motor boat

During the following exercise, we will create an ocean and make geometry into a motor boat using the Make Motor Boats menu option. Then using the attributes found in the Extra Attributes section of the motor boat locator, we will animate the boat across the ocean surface.

Motor boat generating wake

1 Open MotorBoat_Start.mb

- From the *scenes* directory on the Support Files DVD-ROM, open the file named *MotorBoat_Start.mb*.

2 Create the water surface

- In the Dynamics menu set, select **Fluid Effects** → **Ocean** → **Create Ocean** - ❏ and set the following:

    Create Preview Plane to **On**;

    Preview Plane Size to **100**.

- Click on **Create Ocean**.

3 Make the boat geometry into a motor boat

- Select the boat body in the Perspective view and then press the up arrow key on your keyboard to select the *Boat* group node.

- In the Dynamics menu set, select **Fluid Effects** → **Ocean** → **Make Motor Boats**. This will create a dynamically charged locator (with a built-in expression), to which the *Boat* group node will be parented.

Note: If you want to animate the X and Y position of the motor boat across the water surface through keyframing and not by using the locator attributes, turn on Free Transform in the Make Motor Boats options window before applying it to the geometry.

---

4 Adjust the locator's Extra Attributes

- Select **Window** → **Hypergraph...** and select the *locatorShape1* node (to which the Boat is parented).

- Open the **Extra Attributes** section found in the Attribute Editor window for the *locatorShape1* node.

- Press the **Play** button in the animation controls found in the right bottom corner of Maya's user interface window.

- Set the **Buoyancy** to **0.700**.

    Lowering the buoyancy, you will sink the boat deeper into the water. The Air and Water Damping models the effects of friction and viscosity of the air on the object's motion.

- For natural motion, set the **Boat Length** and the **Boat Width** equal to the actual length and width values (measured grid units).

    The **Roll** sets the rolling motion of the boat from side to side.

    The **Pitch** sets the pitching motion of the boat so that the front end rises or falls in relation to the back end. We will leave these attributes to their default values for now.

5 Animate the Boat

- Open the **Extra Attributes** section in the Attribute Editor for *locatorShape1*.

- Start increasing the **Throttle** value while the simulation is playing and you will see the boat starting to move across the water. This attribute sets the velocity of the boat, comparable to opening or closing the throttle in a boat. Set the **Throttle** value to **6.000**.

  The **Rudder** sets the angle of the rudder to make the boat turn. Change the **Rudder** value to a positive value and the boat will start turning towards its left. If you choose a negative value it will turn the boat towards its right. You can leave this value to zero for now or change it as you please.

- Set the **Throttle Pitch** to **11.282**. This attribute sets how much the front of the boat rises when the throttle is "open".

  You could keyframe the **Rudder** attribute value from negative to positive in order to change the direction of the boat in a zigzag type of motion.

- **Save** your work.

Note: The Turn Roll attribute sets how much the boat rolls to the side as it turns. This attribute has no effect if the Rudder attribute is set to zero.

Making shelf buttons for an interactive boat simulation

MEL shelf buttons can be created for a more interactive boat simulation. To make one of the following MEL script examples into a shelf button, you have to type the script into the Inputs section of the Script Editor window and then after you highlight it, MMB drag it onto the shelf. While you playback the simulation you can use the shelf buttons to modify the way the boat will move across the water's surface.

MEL button examples:

1 Increase Throttle

```
float $t = `getAttr locator1.throttle`;
setAttr locator1.throttle ($t + 0.5);
```

2 Decrease Throttle

```
float $t = `getAttr locator1.throttle`;
$t -= 0.5;
```

```
if( $t < 0 ) $t = 0.0;
setAttr locator1.throttle $t;
```

3 Rudder Left

```
float $t = `getAttr locator1.rudder`;
$t += 2.0;
if( $t > 20 ) $t = 20;
setAttr locator1.rudder $t;
```

4 Rudder Right

```
float $t = `getAttr locator1.rudder`;
$t -= 2.0;
if( $t < -20 ) $t = -20;
setAttr locator1.rudder $t;
```

5 Stop Boat

```
setAttr locator1.throttle 0;
setAttr locator1.rudder 0;
```

Adding wake and foam to the boat

In this exercise, we will continue working on the scene saved in the previous exercise. We will add a wake and foam to the motor boat simulation. This will create two 3D fluid containers (used as textures) and an emitter that will interact with the ocean surface by overidding the Wave Height Offset and respectively the Foam Offset of the *oceanShader1* node. The intensity of the wake effect can be adjusted by either modifying the values for the Density/ Voxel/Sec of the *OceanWakeEmitter1*, or by adjusting the Density attributes of the *OceanWakeTexture1* (found in the Contents Details section of the Attribute Editor). The intensity of the foam emission can be adjusted by either modifying the values for Heat/Voxel/Sec of the *OceanWakeEmitter1*, or by adjusting the Temperature attributes of the *OceanWakeFoamTexture1* also found in the Contents Details section of the Attribute Editor.

1 Open FoamAndWake_Start.mb

- From the *scenes* directory on the Support Files DVD-ROM open the file named *FoamAndWake_Start.mb*, or use the file that you saved at the end of the previous exercise.

2 Add wake and foam to the boat

- Open **Window → Hypergraph...** and select the *locator1* node (to which the *Boat* is parented).

- In the Dynamics menu set, select **Fluid Effects → Ocean → Create Wake -** ❑ and set the following:

  Wake Size to **100**;

  Wake Intensity to **3**;

  Foam Creation to **3**.

- Click **Create Ocean Wake**.

  This will create two 3D containers, one for the wake and the other for the foam emission.

3 Adjust the Preview Plane Resolution

- In the Perspective view, select the ocean **Preview Plane** and open the Attribute Editor window.

- Set the **Resolution** to **40**.

  This will allow you to get a better preview quality for the wake and foam effects.

4 Adjust the shape and position of the wake emitter

- Open **Window → Hypergraph...** and select the *OceanWakeEmitter1* node (parented to the *locator1* node).

- Open the Attribute Editor and in the **Volume Emitter Attributes** section set the **Volume Shape** to **Cone**.

- In the Channel Box, adjust the emitter transform attributes as follows:

  Rotate Z to **90**;

  Translate X to **-7**;

  Scale Y to **4**;

  Scale Z to **3**.

5 Tweak the results

- If you want to tweak the wake and foam effects you can do so by adjusting the Density content of the *OceanWakeTexture1* node or the Temperature content of the *OceanWakeFoamTexture1* node under the **Contents Details** section of the Attribute Editor.

6 Save your work

Overview of ponds

Ponds are in fact 2D fluids that use a spring mesh solver and a height field to generate the water simulation. They are better suited for creating smaller bodies of water. The Pond menu items function in almost the same manner as the Ocean menu items. You can float objects using the same instructions from the Oceans section of this chapter. As opposed to oceans, when you create wake and foam for a floating object, no new fluid containers get created, but an emitter will be created that will affect the Pond fluid.

The following emitter attributes control wake behavior:

- **Density/Voxel/Sec** controls the wake intensity.

- **Heat/Voxel/Sec** controls foam creation if the Temperature Method on the pond is set to Dynamic Grid.

The appearance of the pond surface can be modified using the pond options and attributes. You can set the Size, Resolution, Color, and Transparency of your fluid surface the same way as for any other 2D fluid container.

To create wakes in a Pond fluid:

- Select the object you want to create a wake for and **Shift-select** the Pond.

- In the Dynamics menu set select **Fluid Effects** → **Pond** → **Create Wake** - ☐.

- Set the wake options. The **Wake Intensity** will set the emission value for the **Density/Voxel/Sec** attributes of the *PondWakeEmitter*. The **Foam Creation**, if different than zero, will set the Temperature content of the Pond fluid to Dynamic Grid, and will set the emission value for the **Heat/Voxel/Sec** attributes of the *PondWakeEmitter*.

Stone falling into the water

Within the following exercise, we will use a Pond wake to simulate the effect of a stone falling into the water. The stone geometry will be made into an Active Rigid Body and a Gravity field will be used to make it fall into the water.

1 Create the water surface

- In the Dynamics menu set, select **Fluid Effects** → **Pond** → **Create Pond** - ☐.

- Set the **Size** to **40** and click on the **Create Pond** button.

2 Create the stone geometry

- In the **Create** menu select **NURBS Primitives** → **Sphere**.

- In the Channel Box, rename the sphere to *Stone*.

3 Create the wake for the Stone

- Select the *Stone* node and **Shift-select** the Pond fluid.

- In the Dynamics menu set, select **Fluid Effects** → **Pond** → **Create Wake** - ❑.

- Set the **Wake Intensity** to **2** and click on the **Create Wake** button.

4 Make the Stone into an Active Rigid Body

- Select the *Stone* and move it above the Pond surface about 17 units.

- With the *Stone* geometry selected, in the Dynamics menu set select **Soft/Rigid Bodies** → **Create Active Rigid Body**.

5 Add Gravity to the Stone

- Select the *Stone* and in the Dynamics menu set select **Fields** → **Gravity**.

6 Playback the simulation

- Set your playback end to **300** in the timeline preferences.

- Using the playback controls in the timeline, play your simulation.

Conclusion

Fluid containers allow you to create a wide variety of 2D and 3D effects (e.g. atmospheric effects, pyrotechnic effects, etc.), affect geometry, cloth, or particles. Using Ocean shaders or Ponds, you can create open water effects, float objects, create motor boats, and add wake and foam to the simulation.

In this chapter, the following topics were covered:

- Atmospheric effects with 2D and 3D fluid containers;

- Pyrotechnic effects such as smoke fire and explosions;

- Affecting geometry, cloth, and particles with fluids;

- Fluids as textures;

- Open water effects using Ocean shaders and Ponds;

- Floating objects with wake and foam.

2 Maya Fur

Maya Fur is a great tool for creating fur on animals. In this next chapter, you will create fur for a multi-surface NURBS model. The fur will then be modified and fine-tuned to simulate realistic animal fur.

In this chapter, you will learn how to:

- Work with fur on a multi-surface NURBS model;
- Offset fur so all patches flow in the same general direction;
- Work with the Fur Paint Tool to comb the direction of the fur;
- Work with the Fur Paint Tool to modify the length of the fur;
- Apply color to the Base and Tip Color attributes of a Fur Description;
- Fine-tune fur descriptions;
- Add fur shading effects for additional realism;
- Define how fur renders using the Fur Render Globals.

APPLYING FUR TO A PATCH MODEL

The model of this hamster consists of several NURBS patches. Quick selection sets have already been created for easy selection of the hamster's body, ears, eyes and toes.

Before you start this lesson, copy the project folder called *HamsterProject* into your Maya project folder located on your hard drive.

> For example:
> *C:\Documents and Settings\My Documents\maya\projects\HamsterProject*

1 Create a Fur Description

- Open the file called *HermanStart.mb*.

  The hamster model is made up of NURBS patches. 3D textures have been painted to color the surface and fur has already been created for the hamster's ears.

  Sections of the hamster model have been put into Display layers and Quick Select Sets were created to quickly switch between common selections.

- In the Display Layer Editor, turn **Off** visibility for the *LftEarLayer* and *RgtEarLayer*.

- Select **Edit → Quick Selection Sets → HeadSet**
  to quickly select the surfaces that belong to the hamster's head.

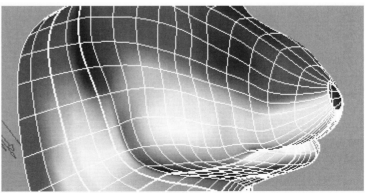

HeadSet selected

- Select **Fur → Attach Fur Description → New**.

Maya Fur creates a fur description and attaches it to the selected surfaces. Fur Feedback automatically displays on the selected surfaces, providing you with a visual representation of the default fur attributes for the fur description.

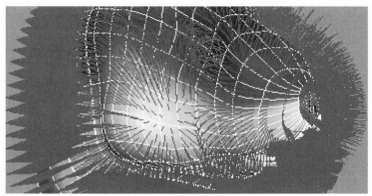

Fur Description attached

2 Rename FurDescription

Changing the names of the fur description and *FurFeedback* nodes to something meaningful is useful for easy identification if more than one fur description is created.

- Select **Fur → Edit Fur Description → FurDescription1**.
- In the Attribute Editor, rename *FurDescription1* to *HeadFur*.

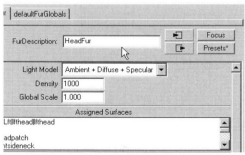

FurDescription1 renamed to HeadFur

Note: There are two fur descriptions present called *LftEarFur* and *RgtEarFur* that have already been created for Herman's ears.

3 Fur Feedback

- In the Outliner, set **Display** → **Shapes** to **On**.
- Expand the *FurFeedback* node.

  Note that there is a *FurFeedback* display node for each surface with the HamHead Quick Selection Set.

- Select each *FurFeedback* within the top *FurFeedback* node.

All FurFeedback nodes selected within the top FurFeedback node

- Open the Channel Box. Under **Shapes**, set the following:

  U Samples to **8**;

  V Samples to **8**;

  Fur Accuracy to **1**;

  Color Feedback Enable to **On**.

Note: The number of U and V Samples on the surface determines how many feedback hairs display. However, this does not change how many hairs actually render on the surface.

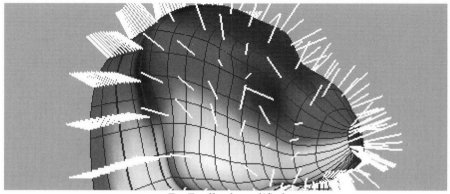

FurFeedback modified

Fur Accuracy sets how closely the *FurFeeedback* resembles the appearance of the final rendered fur. Fur Accuracy ranges from 0 to 1. A value of 0 represents the hairs as straight lines while a value of 1 will give a good indication of what the final fur render will look like, but it can slow interaction.

4 Rename FurFeedback node

- In the Outliner, select the *FurFeedback* node.
- Rename the *FurFeedback* node to *HeadFurFeedback*.

Tip: It is better to decrease the U and V Samples on very small surfaces so you can see the effect of fur attributes more clearly while you work.

---

5 Reverse Fur Normals

By default, when you attach fur to a model, each hair making up the fur points in a direction normal (perpendicular) to the surface. This direction is called the fur normal.

If your model appears to have very short fur after you attached a fur description to it, it could be because the fur normal is pointing in the negative direction.

To solve this problem, you must reverse the fur normals. The fur will point out from the surface rather than into the model.

- In the Outliner, select the *HamsterLft* node and expand.
- Select *lfthead* and expand.
- Select the *lftmouth* node.

lftmouth node selected

- Select **Fur → Reverse Fur Normals**.

Fur normals reversed

- In the Outliner, select the *HamsterRgt* node and expand.
- Select the *head* node and expand.
- Select the *rgtmouth* node.
- Select the *fronttorso* top node and expand.
- **Ctrl-select** the following surfaces:

    rgtlowsidetorso;

    rgtlowfronttorso;

    rgtlowfacetorso.

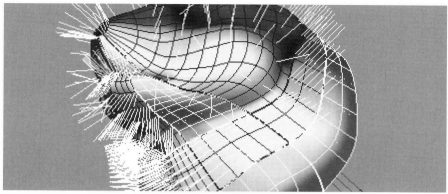

Reversed fur

- Select **Fur → Reverse Fur Normals**.

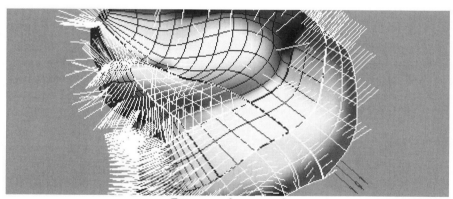

Fur normals reversed

6 Edit HeadFur Description

When you edit a fur description, any changes you make to the fur attributes apply to all surfaces that are assigned to the fur description.

- Select **Fur → Edit Fur Description → HeadFur**.

    Set the following values:

    Length to **0.80**;

    Inclination to **0.85**;

    Roll to **0.8**;

    Base Curl to **0.75**;

    Tip Curl to **0.55**.

Edited HeadFur Description

7 Offset HeadFur Direction

When you add fur to a model and adjust the Inclination, Polarity, and Roll, you may find that the fur grows in different directions for some of the surfaces.

The direction fur grows in is determined by the Inclination of the fur (how much the fur sticks out), the Polarity of the fur (the angle each hair rotates around the fur normal), and the Roll of the fur (the angle each hair rotates about the surface V-axis).

- In the Outliner, select the *HamsterLft* node and expand.
- Select the *lfthead* node.

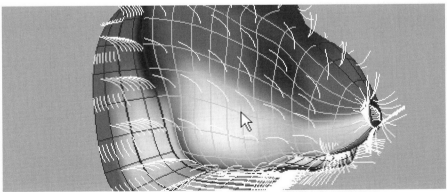

Fur direction incorrect

- Select **Fur** → **Offset Fur Direction by** → **270 Degrees**.

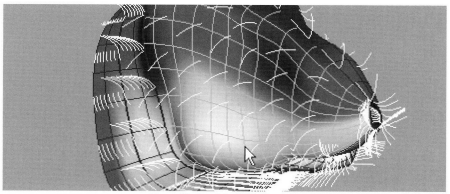

Fur offset set to 270 degrees

- With the *lfthead* node still selected, expand.
- Select the *lftsideneck* node.

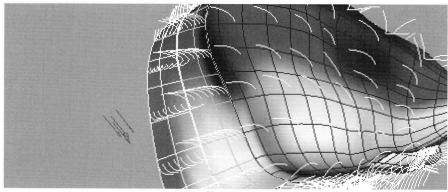

Fur offset incorrect

- Select **Fur → Offset Fur Direction by → 270 Degrees**.
- Select the *lftfronttorso* node and expand.
- Select the *lftlowsidetorso* node.
- Select **Fur → Offset Fur Direction by → 270 Degrees**.

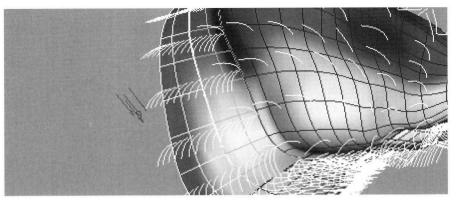

Fur offsetset set to 270 degrees

- In the Outliner, select the *lfthead* node and the *lftfronttorso* node groups and expand.
- **Ctrl-select** the following nodes:

  lftlowfrontsideneck;

  lftlowfrontneck;

  lftlowfronttorso;

  lftlowfacetorso.

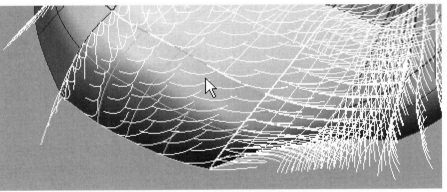

Fur direction incorrect

Select **Fur → Offset Fur Direction by → 180 Degrees.**

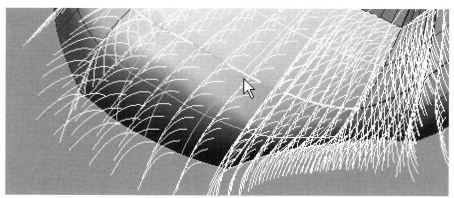

Fur offset set to180 degrees

- In the Outliner, select the *HamsterRgt* node and expand.
- Select the *head* node and expand.
- Select the *rgtsideneck* node.

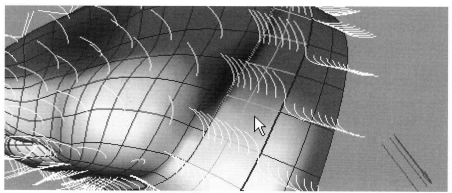

Fur direction incorrect

- Select **Fur → Offset Fur Direction by → 180 Degrees**.

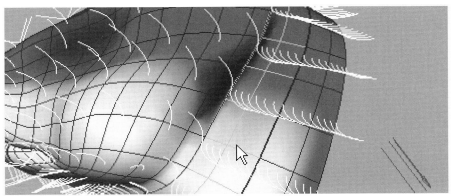

Fur offset set to180 degrees

- With the *HamsterRgt / Head* node still expanded, select the *rgtsideheadpath* node.

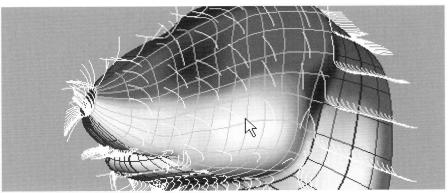

Fur direction incorrect

- Select **Fur → Offset Fur Direction by → 180 Degrees**.

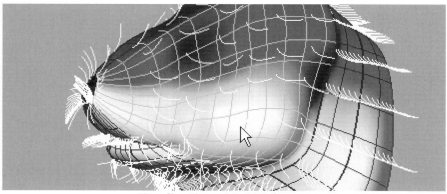

Fur direction set to 180 degrees

Comb fur

1 Paint Direction for HeadFur Description

To comb fur, you will paint the direction of fur using the **Paint Fur Attributes Tool**.

The direction we comb sets the **Polar** attribute value to correspond with the direction we are painting, and as a result, a map will be created for the **Polar** attribute.

- Select **Edit** → **Quick Select Sets** → **HeadSet**.

- Select **Fur** → **Paint Fur AttributesTool - ❑**.

   The Paint Fur Attributes Tool Settings window opens, followed by the Paint Scripts Tool Attribute Editor.

Paint Fur Attributes Tool Settings window

- In the Paint Fur Attributes Tool Settings window, set the following:

   Fur Attribute to **Direction**;

   Fur Description to **HeadFur**.

   When painting, make sure the correct attribute you want to paint is selected next to **Fur Attribute**. In this case, the fur attribute that we want to paint is **Direction**.

Note: Only the fur descriptions attached to the selected surfaces are available for selection.

Attribute Map Width to **256**;

Attribute Map Height to **256**.

- Close the window.

Tip: The Attribute Map should be twice as large as the number of U and V Samples, or detail will be lost for attributes that will be painted using the **Paint Attributes Tool**.

2 Viewing the Value Map while you paint

While you paint on a surface with an Artisan Tool, you can view the greyscale Fur Attribute Value Map as you paint. This provides useful feedback when the changes you are painting are not easily detected with the FurFeedback. Keep in mind that this option may slow performance.

- In the Paint Scripts Tool Attribute Editor, open the **Display** section.
- Set **Color Feedback** to **On**.

Color Feedback set to On

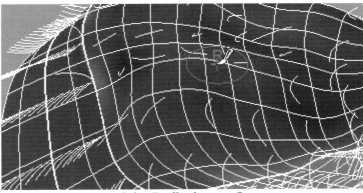

Color Feedback set to On

- In the Paint Scripts Tool Attribute Editor, expand the **Brush** section and set **Opacity** to **1.0**.

- In the **Paint Attributes** section, set the following:

    Paint Operation to **Replace**;

    Value to **0**.

- **Click-drag** the brush across the surface to comb the fur.

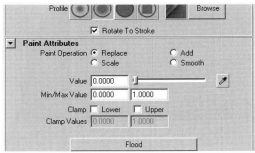

Script Paint Tool Settings

Because the Polar values are affected only by the direction you comb (paint direction), when you comb hair, none of the setting in the Script Paint Tool Editor are relevant. For example, using Smooth is the same as using Replace, and the Value of 1 is the same as the Value of 0.

Tip: To increase the size of the Artisan Paint Brush, hold down the B key on the keyboard or increase the value for Radius (U) and Radius (L) in the Script Paint Tool Settings window.

Note: You can restore the fur direction of the fur description values by deleting the Polar Attribute Map created when you painted the direction. The map is located in the HeadFur Description Attribute Editor in the **Details** section under **Polar → Maps**. While holding the **Ctrl** key, select all surfaces listed under the Surface tab and click on the **Remove Item** button.

Apply fur to MidTorso

You will apply a fur description to the remaining surfaces of the hamster. The fur will also be combed using the previous outlined workflow.

1 Create a Fur Description

- Open the scene file called *HermanStart1.mb*.
- In the Layer Editor, set **Visibility** to **On** for the *MidTorsoLayer*.

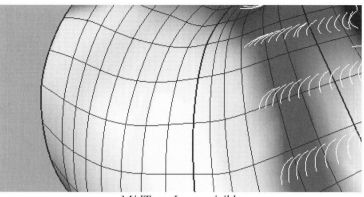

MidTorsoLayer visible

- Select **Edit → Quick Select Sets → MidTorsoSet**.
- Select **Fur → Attach Fur Description → New**.

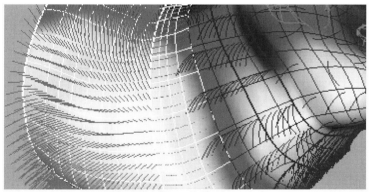

New FurDescription created

- Select **Fur → Edit FurDescription1**.
- In the Attribute Editor, rename *FurDescription* 1 to *MidTorsoFur*.

2 Modify FurFeedback

- In the Outliner, select the new *FurFeedback* node and expand.
- Select all the *FurFeedback* nodes under the new top *FurFeedback* node.

All FurFeedback nodes selected

- In the Channel Box under *shapes*, set the following:

    U Samples to **8**;

    V Samples to **8**;

    Fur Accuracy to **1**;

    Color Feedback Enable to **On**.

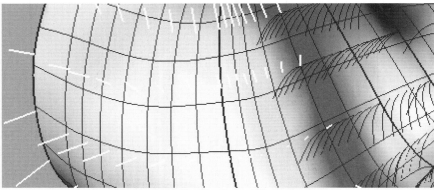

FurFeedback modified

3 Rename FurFeedback node

- In the Outliner, select the new *FurFeedback* node.
- Rename the *FurFeedback* node to *MidTorsoFurFeedback*.

4 Reverse Fur Normals

Reverse the hairs on the surfaces that appear to face inward.

- In the Outliner, select the *HamsterLft* node and expand.

- Select the *lftfronttorso* node and expand.
- Select the *lftmidTorso* node and expand.
- **Ctrl-select** the following nodes from both group nodes:

    lftuppersidetorso;

    lftlowermidtorso.

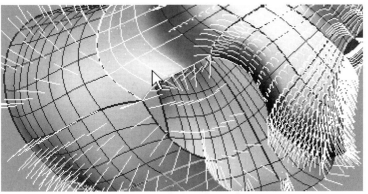

Fur normals inside surface

- Select **Fur → Reverse Fur Normals**.

Fur normals reversed

- In the Outliner, select the *HamsterRgt* node and expand.
- Select the *rgtMidTorso* node and expand.
- Select the following nodes:

    rgtlowmidtorso;

    rftupperSideMidtorso.

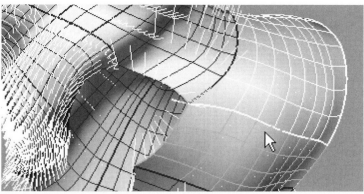

Fur normals inside surface

Select **Fur** → **Reverse Fur Normals**.

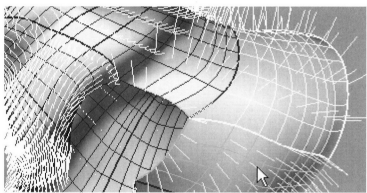

Fur normals reversed

5 Modify Mid Torso Fur Attributes

- Select **Fur** → **Edit Fur Description** → **MidTorsoFur**.
- Set the following values:

    Inclination to **9.0**;

    Roll to **0.8**;

    Base Curl to **0.70**;

    Tip Curl to **0.55**.

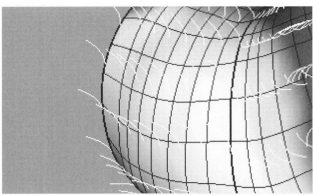

MidTorso FurDescription modified

6 Offset Direction of MidTorso FurDescription

- In the Outliner, select the *HamsterLft* node and expand.

- Select the *lftmidTorso* node and expand.

- Select the *lftlowmidtorso* node.

- Select **Fur → Offset Fur Direction by → 180 Degrees**.

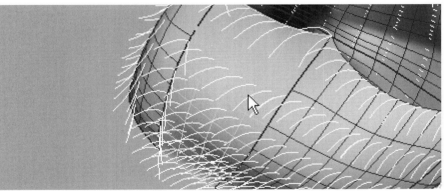

Fur offset to 180 degrees

- Still within the *HamsterLft/lftmidTorso*, select the *lftupperSideMidtorso* node.

- Select **Fur → Offset Fur Direction by → 90 Degrees**.

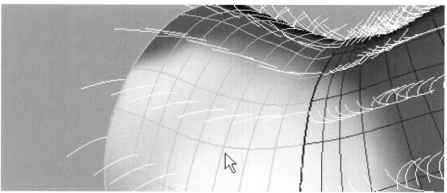

Fur offset to 90 degrees

- Within the *HamsterLft/lftmidTorso*, select the *lftlowermidtorso* node.
- Select **Fur → Offset Fur Direction by → 180 Degrees**.

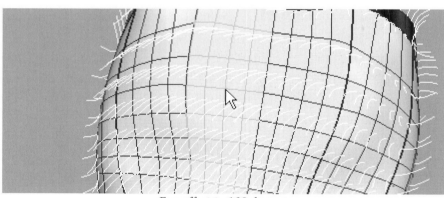

Fur offset to 180 degrees

- In the Outliner, select the *HamsterRgt* node and expand.
- Select the *rgtMidTorso* node and expand.
- Select the *rgtupperSideMidTorso* node.
- Select **Fur → Offset Fur Direction by → 180 Degrees**.

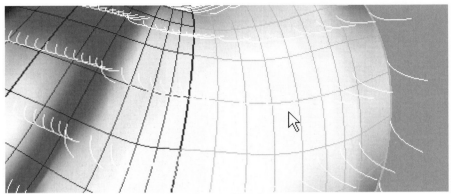

Fur offset to 180 degrees

Comb fur

1 Paint direction for MidTorso Fur Description

- Select **Edit** → **Quick Select Sets** → **MidTorsoSet**.
- Select **Fur** → **Paint Fur Attributes Tool** - ❑.

  The Paint Fur Attributes Tool Settings window opens, followed by the Paint Scripts Tool Attribute Editor.

- Set the following in the Paint Fur Attributes Tool Settings window:

  Fur Attribute to **Direction**;

  Fur Description to **MidTorsoFur**;

  Attribute Map Width to **256**;

  Attribute Map Height to **256**.

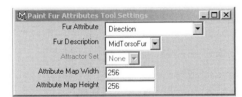

Paint Fur Attributes Tool Settings window

- Close the window.
- In the Paint Scripts Tool Attribute Editor, expand the **Brush** section and set **Opacity** to **1.0**.

- In the **Paint Attributes** section, set the following:

    Paint Operation to **Replace**;

    Value to **0**.

- **Click-drag** the brush across the surface to comb the fur.

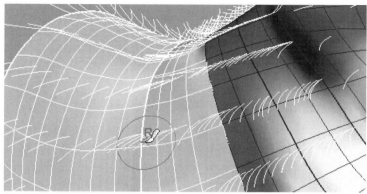

MidTorso fur combed

Apply what you have learned so far to the remaining sections of the hamster, *backTorso* and *tail*. Make visible the *BackTorso* layer and the *BackTail* layer. Also, select the appropriate Quick Select Sets.

Make sure to set FurDescription attribute values, such as Inclination, Roll, Base and Tip Curl before combing the direction of fur.

Create fur for the hamster's front and back legs

1 Create a Fur Description

You will create a fur description for the hamster's back legs.

- Open the scene called *HermanStart2.mb*.

- Using the Layer Editor, turn visibility **On** for the layer called *BackLegLayer*.

- Turn visibility **Off** for the following layers:

    HeadLayer;

    MidTorsoLayer;

    BackTorsoLayer;

    BackTailLayer.

BackLegLayer is untemplated

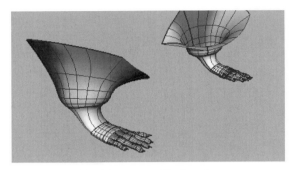

BackLegLayer displayed

- Select **Edit → Quick Select Sets → BackLftLegSet**.
- Select **Fur → Attach Fur Description → New**.

FurDescription1 attached

- Select **Fur → Edit FurDescription1**.
- In the Attribute Editor, rename *FurDescription1* to *BkLftLegFur*.

2 Reverse Fur Normals

Reverse the hairs on the surfaces that appear to be facing inward.

- In the Outliner, select the *HamsterLft node* and expand.

- Select the *lftbackLeg* node and expand.
- Select the following nodes:

  lftbackleg2;

  lftbackleg3;

  lftlowbackLeg1;

  lftlowbackLeg2;

  lftbottomBackLeg;

  lftbottomBackLeg1.

Fur inversed

- Select **Fur → Reverse Fur Normals**.

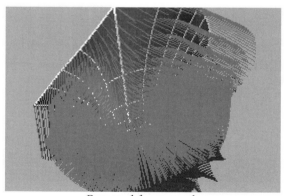

Reversed fur normals

3 Modify FurFeedback

- In the Outliner, select the new *FurFeedback* node and expand.
- Select all the *FurFeedback* nodes with the top *FurFeedback* node.

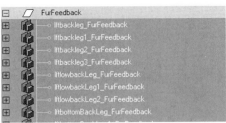

FurFeedback nodes selected

- In the Channel Box under **Shapes**, set the following:

    U Samples to **8**;

    V Samples to **8**;

    Fur Accuracy to **1**;

    Color Feedback Enable to **On**.

4   Rename FurFeedback node

- In the Outliner, select the new *FurFeedback* node.

- Rename the second *FurFeedback* node to *LftBckLegFurFeedback*.

5   Modify attributes for BkLftLeg FurDescription

- Select **Fur** → **Edit Fur Description** → **BkLftLegFur**.

- Set the following values:

    Length to **0.2**;

    Inclination to **0.90**;

    Roll to **0.55**;

    Base Curl to **0.70**;

    Tip Curl to **0.55**.

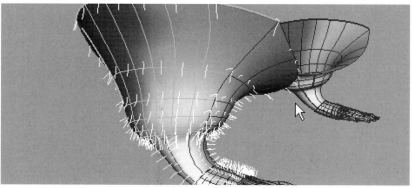

Fur direction incorrect

6 Offset Fur Direction

- In the Outliner, select the *HamsterLft* node and expand.
- Select the *lftbackLeg* node and expand.
- Select the *lftbackleg2* node.
- Select **Fur → Offset Fur Direction by → 90 Degrees**.

Fur offset to 90 degrees

- Within the *lftbackleg* top node, continue to select the following nodes:

  lftbottomBackLeg ;

  lftbottomBackLeg1.

- Select **Fur → Offset Fur Direction by → 90 Degrees**.

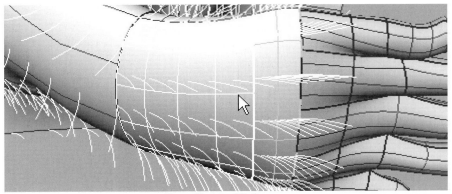

Fur offset to 90 degrees

- Within the *lftbackleg top* node, continue to select the following nodes:

    lftlowbackLeg1;

    lftlowbackLeg2;

- Select **Fur → Offset Fur Direction by → 270 Degrees**.

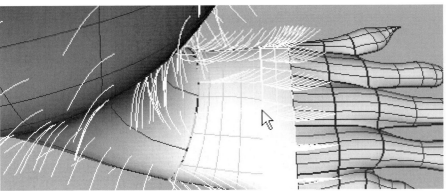

Fur offset to 270 degrees

Comb fur

1 Paint direction for BackLeg Fur Descriptions

- Select **Edit → Quick Select Sets → LgtBackLegSet**.

- Select **Fur → Paint Fur Attributes Tool - ❑**.

    The Paint Fur Attributes Tools Settings window opens followed by the Paint Scripts Tool Attribute Editor.

- Set the following in the Paint Fur Attributes Tool Settings window:

    Fur Attribute to **Direction**;

    Fur Description to **BkRgtLegFur**;

    Attribute Map Width to **256**;

    Attribute Map Height to **256**.

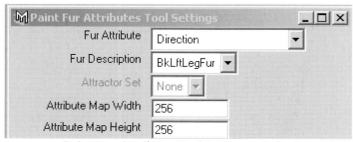

Paint Fur Attributes Tool Settings window

- Close window.
- In the Paint Scripts Tool Attribute Editor, expand the **Brush** section:

    Set Opacity to **1.0**.

- In the **Paint Attributes** section, set the following:

    Paint Operation to **Replace**;

    Value to **0**.

- **Click-drag** the brush across the surface to comb the fur.

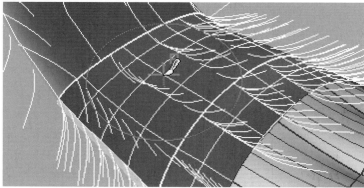

Comb fur

- Apply the same workflow to right back Leg of the hamster. Make sure to select the *BackRgtLegSet* Quick Select Set.

Apply fur to the front legs of the hamster

1 Create a Fur Description

Now you will apply fur to the front legs of the hamster

- Open the scene *HermanStart3.mb.*

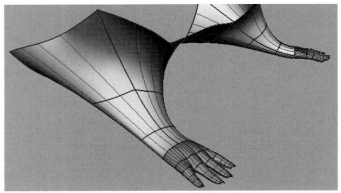

FrontLegLayer displayed

- Select **Edit → Quick Select Sets → FrontLeftLegSet**.
- Select **Fur → Attach Fur Description → New**.

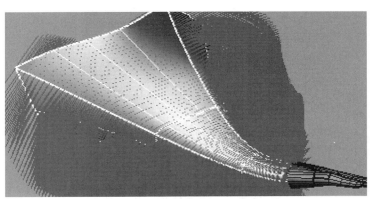

Fur normals inversed

- Select **Edit → Edit Fur Description → FurDescription1**.
- Rename *FurDescription2* to *LftFrontLegFur*.

2 Reverse Fur Normals

Reverse the hairs on the surfaces that appear to be facing inward.

- Select the *HamsterLft* node and expand.

- Select the *lftFrontLeg* node and select the following surfaces:

    lftfrontleg;

    lftfrontleg5;

    lftfrontleg9.

- Select **Fur → Reverse Fur Normals.**

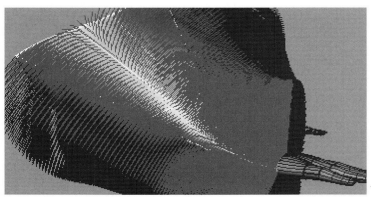

Fur normals reversed

3 Modify FurFeedback

- Select the new *FurFeedback* node in the Outliner and expand.
- Select the *FurFeedback* nodes within the *FurFeedback* top node.

FurFeedback nodes selected

- Set the following under the **Shapes** section:

    U Samples to **8**;

    V Samples to **8**;

    Fur Accuracy to **1**;

    Color Feedback Enable to **On**.

- Select the *FurFeedback* node in the Outliner.

- Rename the new *FurFeedback* node to *LftFrontLegFurFeedback*.

4   Adjust LftFrontLegFur description

- Select **Fur → Edit Fur Description → LftFrontLegFur**.

- Set the following values:

    Length to **0.3**;

    Inclination to **0.8**;

    Roll to **0.6**;

    Base Curl to **0.70**;

    Tip Curl to **0.55**.

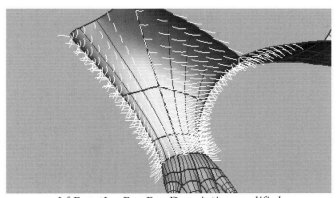

LftFrontLegFur Fur Description modified

Comb fur

1   Paint direction for LftFrontLegFur Description

- Select **Edit → Quick Select Sets → FrontLeftLegSet**.

- Select **Fur → Paint Fur Attributes Tool - □**.

    The Paint Fur Attributes Tools Settings window opens followed by the Paint Scripts Tool Attribute Editor.

- Set the following in the Paint Fur Attributes Tool Settings window:

    Fur Attribute to **Direction**;

    Fur Description to **LftFrontLegFur**;

    Attribute Map Width to **256**;

    Attribute Map Height to **256**.

Paint Fur Attributes Tool Settings window

- Close window.
- In the Paint Scripts Tool Attribute Editor, expand the **Brush** section:

    Set **Opacity** to **1.0**.

- In the **Paint Attributes** section, set the following:

    Paint Operation to **Replace**;

    Value to **0**.

- **Click-drag** the brush across the surface to comb the fur.

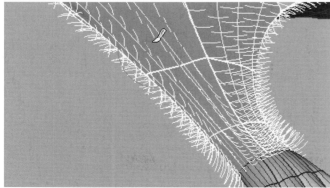

Comb LftFrontLegFur Description

■ Apply the same workflow to the right front leg of the hamster. Make sure to select the *FrontRgtLegSet* Quick Selection Set.

Apply multiple textures to Base and Tip Color of fur

A Lambert material node is assigned to each section of the hamster model. The 3D Paint Tool was used to color each section of the hamster model which created several file textures for each NURBS patch. A *TripleSwitch* Utility node was automatically generated and used to assign each texture to their associating NURBS patch on the hamster model.

The *TripleShadingSwitch* Utility nodes will be mapped into the Base and Tip Color of each FurDescription to color the fur.

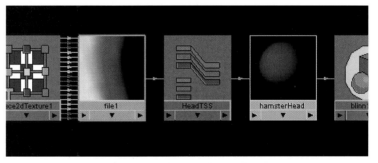

Input and Output Connections of a file texture

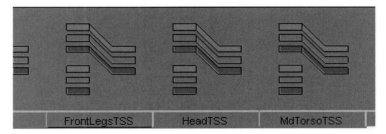

TripleShadingSwitch Utility nodes

1 Map Base and Tip Color of HeadFur Description

■ Open the scene file called *HermanStart4.mb*.

■ In the Perspective view, select **Panels** → **Saved Layouts** → **Hypershade/Outliner/Persp**.

■ In the Outliner, select the *HeadFurFeedback* node and expand.

■ Select all *FurFeedback* nodes within the *HeadFurFeedback* group.

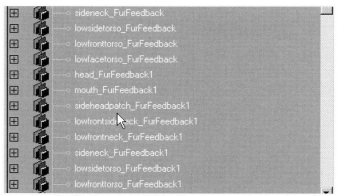

FurFeedback nodes within HeadFurFeedback selected

- In the Hypershade, select the **Utilities** tab.

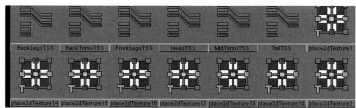

Triple Switch nodes and 2D Placement nodes displayed

- Zoom in until the *HeadTSS* swatch is clearly visible.

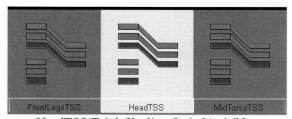

HeadTSS(TripleShading Switch) visible

- Select **Fur → Edit Fur Description → HeadFur**.

  The Attribute Editor will open to show the attributes for *HeadFur*.

- Position the cursor over the *HeadTSS* and with the **MMB-drag** and drop it over the **Base Color** attribute in the HeadFur Description Attribute Editor.

Note:	A black outline in the shape of a rectangle will appear before the connection is made between the Head Fur Base Color attribute and the HeadTSS triple switch swatch.

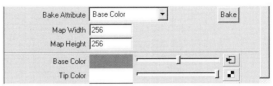

Base Color connected to HeadTSS

- Select the down arrow next to **Bake Attribute** and select **Base Color**.
- Click the **Bake** button.

HeadTSS baked into Base Color

If you edit the texture after baking, bake the texture again, or your changes will not take effect.

Note:	The FurFeedback will not reflect the mapped attributes until you bake.

Tip:	Open the **Details** section of the Base Color attribute, under Maps, to see Base Color maps and their respective assigned surfaces.

To keep the color of the fur the same from base to tip, we will apply the same method to the Tip Color.

- **Drag+drop** the *HeadTSS* node from the Hypershade into the **Tip Color** Attribute of the HeadFur Description.

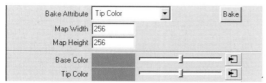
Tip Color connected to HeadTSS

- Select the drop down menu next to the **Bake Attribute** and select **Tip Color**.

- Click the **Bake** button.

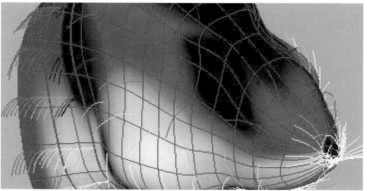
HeadTSS baked into Tip Color

2 Map Base and Tip Color of MidTorso FurDescription

- In the **Layer Editor**, turn visibility to **On** for the *MidTorsoLayer*.

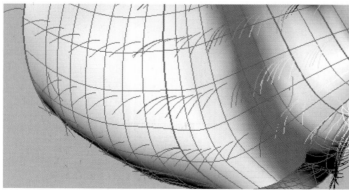
MidTorsoLayer displayed

- Select **Fur → Edit Fur Description → MidTorsoFur.**

- In the Hypergraph, select the **Utility** tab and frame the switch utility node called *MdTorsoTSS*.

Frame MidTorsoTSS

- **Drag+drop** the *MdTorsoTSS* node onto the **Base Color** of the **MidTorsoFur** Description.

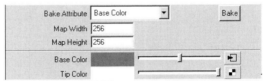

MdTorsoTSS connected Base Color

- Select the down menu next to **Bake Attribute** and select **Base Color**.
- Click the **Bake** button.

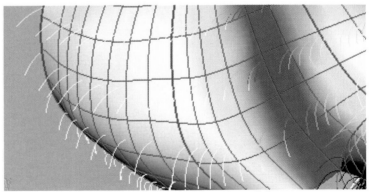

MdTorsoTSS baked into Base Color

- **Drag+drop** the *MdTorsoTSS* node onto the **Tip Color** of the **MidTorsoFur** Description.

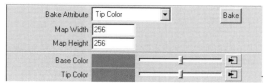

MdTorosTSS connected to Tip Color

- Select the **Tip Color** attribute next to **Bake Attribute**.
- Click the **Bake** button.

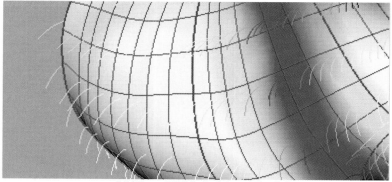

MdTorsoTSS baked into Tip Color

- Apply the above workflow to the remaining sections of the hamster. Make sure the Quick Select Sets match the appropriate Triple Switch Swatch already assigned in the Hypershade.

   BackTorsoSet to *BackTorsoTSS;*

   TailSet to *TailTSS;*

   BkLftLegSet to *BackLegsTSS;*

   BkRgtLegSet to *BackLegsTSS;*

   FrontLftLegSet to *FrontLegsTSS;*

   FrontRgtLegSet to *FrontLegsTSS.*

Paint Length using the Fur Paint Attributes Tool

The Fur Paint Tool will be used to edit the length of the HeadFur Description. You will paint shorter hairs around the eye, mouth and nose area. You will then create whiskers by creating a second fur description for the hamster's head.

1   Increase U and V Samples FurFeedback nodes
   - Open the scene file called *HermanStart5.mb.*

More U and V Samples are required to get more feedback on the patch surfaces.

- In the Outliner, select and expand the *HeadFurFeedback* node.
- **Ctrl-select** each *FurFeedback* node within the *HeadFurFeedback* group node.
- In the Channel Box, set the following:

    U Samples to **25**;

    V Samples to **25**.

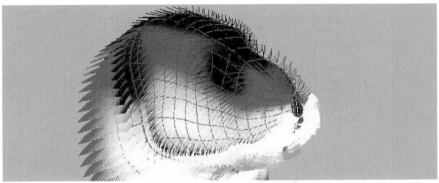

U and V Samples increased

2 **Paint Length around the eyes, nose, mouth and chin**

Hairs are noticeably shorter around a hamster's, eyes, nose and mouth.

- Select **Edit → Quick Select Sets → HeadSet**.
- Select **Fur → Paint Fur Attributes Tool - ❐**.
- Set the following in the Paint Fur Attributes Tool Settings:

    Fur Attribute to **Length**;

    Fur Description to **HeadFur**;

    Attribute Map Width to **256**;

    Attribute Map Height to **256**.

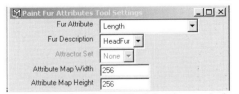

Paint Fur Attributes Tool Settings window

- Close window.
- In the **Brush** section of the Paint Scripts Tool Attribute Editor, set **Opacity** to **1.0**.

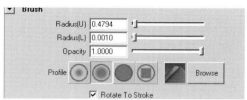
Brush section of Paint Scripts Tool Attribute Editor

- Under Paint Attributes, set the following:

    Paint Operation to **Replace**;

    Value to **0.5** (optional).

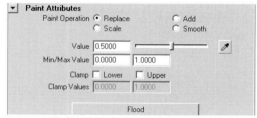
Paint Attributes Values set

Turn on **Reflection** while you paint the eyes, nose and mouth areas.

- Scroll down to the **Stroke** section.
- Set the following:

    Reflection to **On**;

    Reflection Axis to **X**.

Reflection checked On

- Dolly in on the eye, nose, mouth and lower chin.
- Shorten the length of fur around the areas of the eye.

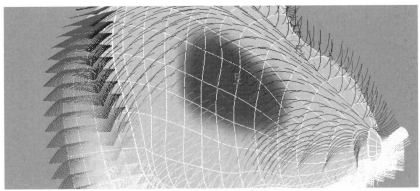

Paint value of 0.3 around the eyes

- Dolly in on the nose, lower mouth, and chin area surfaces.
- In the Paint Scripts Tool Attribute Editor, under the **Stroke** section, turn off **Reflection**.
- In the **Paint Attributes** section, set **Value** to **0.2** (optional).
- Paint around the edge of the nose, mouth and chin.

  Change paint values as necessary while painting to make sure the fur around the edge of the nose, mouth and chin are the shortest.

Painted value of 0.04 around the nose and mouth

Tip:	To change the Brush Radius (U) and Radius (L) values, select the **B** key on the keyboard while you **Click-drag** in the interactive view or manually set values in the Paint Scripts Tool Attribute Editor.

3 Smooth paint values

After you have shortened the length of hairs around the eyes, nose mouth and chin areas, you will smooth out the painted areas for a seamless transition between values:

- In the Paint Scripts Tool Attribute Editor in the **Paint Attributes** section, set **Paint Operation** to **Smooth**.

Smooth paint values

Paint Length on the hamster's back legs

1 Increase U and V Samples FurFeedback nodes

- Open the scene file called *HermanStart6.mb.*
- In the Display Layer Editor, turn **Off** visibility for *HeadLayer.*
- Turn **On** visibility for the *BackLegLayer.*
- In the Outliner, select the *LftBckLegFurFeedback* node and expand.
- Select all *FurFeedback* nodes within the *LftBckLegFurFeedback* and open the Channel Box.

FurFeedback nodes selected within the LftBckLegFurFeedback group

- Set the following:

  U Samples to **20**;

  V Samples to **20**.

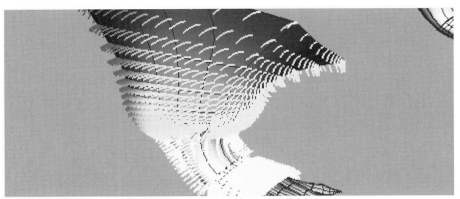

U and V Samples set to 20

- Select **Edit → Quick Select Sets → BckLftLegSet.**
- Select **Fur → Paint Fur Attributes Tool - ❐.**
- Set the following:

   Fur Attribute to **Length**;

   Fur Description to **BkLftLegFur**;

   Attribute Map Width to **256**;

   Attribute Map Height to **256**.

Paint Fur Attributes Tool Settings window

- Close window.
- In the Paint Scripts Tool Attribute Editor under **Brush**, set **Opacity** to **1**
- In the **Paint Attributes** section, set the following:

   Paint Operation to **Replace**;

   Value to **0.56** (optional).

- Paint along the upper section of the left foot.

Paint a value of 0.56 on upper section of the back left foot.

- In the **Paint Attributes** section, set **Value** to **0.35** (optional).
- Paint the middle section of the left back foot.

Paint a value of 0.3 on middle section of the back left foot.

- In the **Paint Attributes** section, set **Value** to **0.05.**
- Paint the lower foot section of the left back foot.

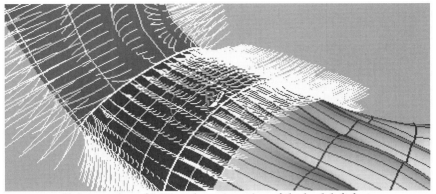

Paint a value of 0.05 on lowest section of the back left foot.

Once you have painted the length values for the left back foot, smooth (Paint Operation to Smooth) out the transition of values along the patches.

- Apply the same workflow to the right back foot of the hamster. Make sure that you select the BckRgtLegSet before painting.

Add whiskers

1 Create a new Fur Description for the hamster head

- Open the scene file *HermanStart7.mb*.
- Select **Edit → Quick Select Sets → Head Set**..
- Select **Fur → Attach Fur Description → New**.

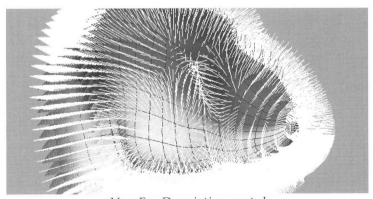

New Fur Description created

- In the Outliner, select the *HeadFurFeedback* node.
- Select **Display → Hide → Hide Selection**.

- Select **Fur** → **Edit Fur Description** → **FurDescription1**.
- In the Attribute Editor, rename *FurDescription1* to *WhiskerFur*.
- In the Outliner select the new *FurFeedback* node and expand.
- Select each *FurFeedback* node within the new *FurFeedback* node.

Select FurFeedback nodes

- In the Channel Box, set the following:

    U Samples to **10**;

    V Samples to **10**;

    Fur Accuracy to **1**;

    Color Feedback Enable to **On**.

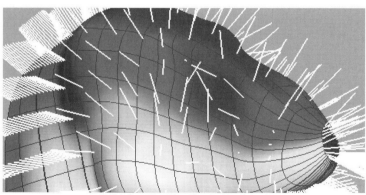

Whisker FurFeedback displayed

- Rename the new *FurFeedback* parent node to *WhiskerFurFeedback*.

2 Paint Baldness for WhiskerFur Description

- Select **Edit** → **Quick Select Sets** → **Head Set**.
- Select **Fur** → **Paint Fur Attributes Tool** - ❑.

- In the Paint Fur Attributes Tool Settings window, set the following:

    Fur Attribute to **Baldness**;

    Fur Description to **WhiskerFur**;

    Attribute Map Width to **256**;

    Attribute Map Height to **256**.

Paint Fur Attributes Tool Settings

- Close window.
- In the Paint Scripts Tool Attribute Editor, in the **Brush** section, set **Opacity** to **1.0**.
- In the **Paint Attributes** section, set the following:

    Paint Operation to **Replace**;

    Value to **0**.

- Click the **Flood** button.

    At this point, no fur should be visible on the hamster's head.

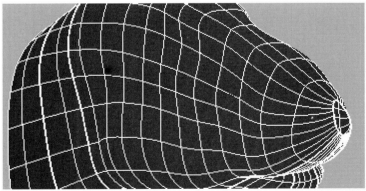

Baldness value of 0

- In the **Paint Attributes** section, set **Value** to **1.0**.
- In the **Scroll** section, set **Reflection** to **On**.
- Paint whiskers on the hamster's cheek pouches.

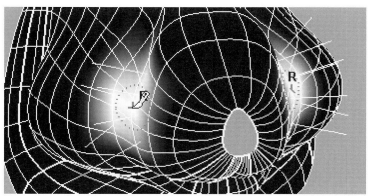

Baldness value of 1 painted to create whiskers

- Exit from the Paint Fur Attributes Tool.

3 Modify WhiskerFur Description

Now we will modify the new WhiskerFur Description for a realistic appearance.

- Open the scene file called *HermanFinal.mb*.

- Select **Fur → Edit Fur Description → WhiskerFur**.

- Set the following attributes for the WhiskerFur Description:

    Density to **150**;

    Tip Color to **0.30**;

Note: The Tip Color value was set by clicking on the color swatch. In the Color Chooser, set the value to 0.30.

Length to **3.0**;

Baldness to **1.0**;

Inclination to **0.3**;

Roll to **0.500**;

Polar to **0.5**;

Base Opacity to **1.0**;

Tip Opacity to **0.800**;

Base Width to **0.030**;

Tip Width to **0.010**;

Base Curl to **1.0**;

Tip Curl to **0.80**;

Scraggle to **0.10**;

Segments to **20**.

Segments defines the number of segments each fur is comprised of. For smoother curves, use more segments. The longer the fur, the more segments are need to produce a smoother result.

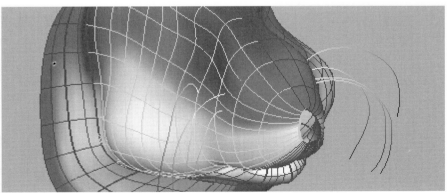

Fur Direction offset for WhiskerFur Description

4 Modify Details section of the WhiskerFur Description

- Scroll down to the **Details** section of the WhiskerFur Description Attribute Editor and expand.

- Expand **Length** and set the following:

    Noise Amplitude to **1.8**;

    Noise Frequency to **12.0**.

- Expand **Inclination** and set the following:

    Noise Amplitude to **0.520**;

    Noise Frequency to **18.0**.

- Expand **Polar** and set the following:

    Noise Amplitude to **0.248**;

    Noise Frequency to **16.0**.

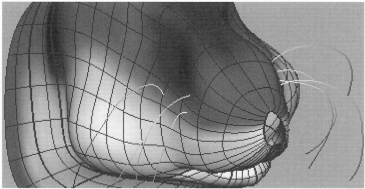

Final result of WhiskerFur Description

- In the Outliner, select the *HeadFurFeedback* node.
- Select **Display → Show → Show Selection**.

    The *HeadFurFeedback* and *WhiskerFurFeedback* will be displayed.

Fine-tune HeadFur Description

At this stage, we will fine-tune each fur description for the hamster body for realism. Frequent renders will be executed to make sure the fur modification is the way we want it.

1 Modify HeadFur Description

- Open the scene file called *HermanFinal.mb*.
- Make all layers invisible except for the *HeadLayer*.
- Select **Fur → Edit Fur Description → HeadFur**.

- Set the following attributes:

    Density to **5000** (optional).

Tip: Start with low density value for faster rendering performance while fine
turning the fur. Before you render increase the **Density Value** so that the
fur fully covers the surfaces.

We do not want a lot of shiny highlights on the fur so we will
lower the **Specular Color** value to **0.2**.

- Select the **Color Swatch** next to **Specular Color**.

    Set **Value** in the color chooser to **0.02**.

    Specular Sharpness to **50**.

The specular sharpness will define the fur highlights. A larger
number yields a sharper and smaller specular highlight.

    Base Opacity to **1.0**;

    Tip Opacity to **0.5**;

    Base Width to **0.020**;

    Tip Width to **0.009**;

    Scraggle to **0.058**;

    Scraggle Frequency to **5.0**;

    Scraggle Correlation to **0**;

    Clumping to **0.08**;

    Clumping Frequency to **0**;

    Clump Shape to **0.05**;

    Segments to **20**;

    Attraction to **1.0**;

    Offset to **0**.

- Expand the **Details** section of the HeadFur Attribute Editor.

- Expand the **Length** section and set the following:

    Noise Amplitude to **1.2**;

    Noise Frequency to **15.0**.

The above values give you a base in fine tuning the hamster's
HeadFur Description. Apply the same settings or your own
values to the remaining hamster fur descriptions.

Tip:	For faster editing and best performance results, it is best to decrease the U and V Samples for each *FurFeedback* node.

Adding fur shading effects

To shade fur that is relatively realistic, we will apply auto-shade lights which can produce self-shading or back shadow effects and takes no longer to render than fur without shading effects.

Most fur roots are not exposed to light. Self-shading simulates this effect by lighting the tips of the fur, and making the roots dark.

Back shadows will simulate the effect of darker regions where the fur does not receive light and lighter regions where the fur is closest to the light.

However, the best way to generate realistic looking shadows onto fur and geometry is by creating fur shadow maps. When we render fur, Maya creates a shadow map for each shadow map light.

Note:	Be aware that although generating several fur shadow maps may produce more realistic results, it takes time and slows rendering. Only spot lights can cast shadows for fur.

Lights have already been set up in the scene. There are four spot lights and one ambient light. We will add Auto-Shade Lighting Attributes to selected spot lights.

1   Set-up a light for fur shading and shadows

- In the Outliner, expand the *Lights* node.

- Select **spotlight1**.

- Select **Fur → Fur Shadowing Attributes → Add To Selected Light**.

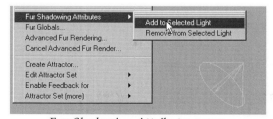

Fur Shadowing Attributes menu

- Open **spotlight1** Attribute Editor.

- Expand **Fur Shading/Shadowing** and adjust the following:

    Fur Shading Type to **Auto-Shading**;

    Self-Shade to **1.0**;

    Self-Shade Darkness to **0.5**;

    Back Shade Factor to **2.5**;

    Back Shade Darkness to **0.3**.

- Render to see results.

    To generate realistic shadows onto fur and geometry, you can create fur shadow maps. A fur shadow map represents depth information generated from the position and orientation of the spot light. The depth information is used to create two types of shadowing, fur shadowing where fur casts shadows on itself and geometry shadowing where fur casts shadows on geometry. In this case, you will use the **Shadow Map** option so the fur will cast shadows on itself.

- Set **Fur Shading Type** to **Shadow Maps.**

- Render to see results.

- Set **Auto-Shade** or **Shadow Map** as the Fur Shading/Shadow technique for the remaining spot lights in the scene.

Note: To cast fur shadows on geometry using spotlights only, expand Shadows and under Depth Map Shadow Attributes, turn on **Use Depth Map Shadows**.

Fur render globals

Fur render globals are the attributes that define how fur renders. These setting must be defined before rendering.

- Select **Fur → Fur Globals.**

    Enable Fur must be turned **On**. If this option is not turned on, the scene renders but the fur is completely ignored and, therefore no fur images will be created.

    Calc. Area Values sets how the fur is distributed across surfaces.

- Since our model is made up of multiple patches, we will set:

    Calc. Area Values to **Globally**.

This option gives an even distribution of hairs across different sized surfaces.

The density of each fur description is distributed evenly over all surfaces with fur descriptions attached, regardless of which fur description is attached.

Fur render globals

Comp. Fur creates a composite of the rendered fur and the rendered models. The fur and the models render separately, but if you turn this option off they are not composited. This option is useful for compositing images using another application.

Keep Temp Files keeps the fur files built by the fur in the process of creating the final fur images. The intermediate files which are fur files and shadow maps are stored in *furFiles* directory and *shadowMap* directory.

If you turn this option off, the intermediate files are deleted when the render is complete. This can stop your disk from filling up with fur files.

Keep Fur Images keeps the fur image files created by fur. These files are useful when you want to turn on **Comp fur**, but still want to see the rendered fur without the model.

- Set **Equalizer Maps** to **Default Equalizer Maps**.

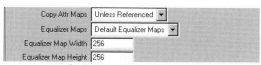

Default Equalizer Maps set

- An equalizer map compensates for the uneven distribution of fur caused by uneven parameterization so that fur is evenly distributed across the surface.

- **Default Equalizer Maps** uses the equalization maps automatically created by fur.

- Open the **Advanced Options** section and set the following:

  Enable Fur Image Rendering to **On**;

  Enable Fur Shading/Shadowing to **On**.

Advanced Options section

- Open the **Fur Image Rendering** section and set the following:

  Hairs/Pixel to **6**;

  Use Fur Shading/Shadowing on Fur to **On**.

Fur Image Rendering options

- Open the **Shadow Map Rendering** section (only if Fur Shading Type is set to Shadow Maps)

  Set **Hairs/Pixel** to **6**.

Shadow Map Rendering options

Conclusion

In this lesson you learned how to create a fur description, and modify the *FurFeedback* node. You offset the fur direction in certain areas of the hamster so that the fur would flow in the proper direction. Then you modified the FurDescriptions and mapped *Triple Switch* nodes assigned to 3D textures to the Base and Tip Color of each FurDescription. Finally, to set up the scene before rendering, you fine-tuned each fur description and applied fur shadowing techniques using spot lights.

3 Maya Hair

Hair Systems use a collection of dynamic NURBS curves that are generated from hair follicles. Each hair follicle contains one NURBS curve, but it can also contain a number of hairs that make up a clump. The follicle has various attributes for modifying the appearance and style of the hair, including a Braid Attribute. The Paint Hair Tool allows for creating and removing follicles, as well as painting hair attributes, including Clump Width Scale, Stiffness, and Braid. With hair, you can simulate natural movement of long hair, hair blowing in the wind, hair motion when swimming underwater and various hair styles including braids and updos. Since hair is a generic Dynamic Curve simulation, the curves can also be used to create non-hair effects such as sea creatures and suspension bridges. In this chapter you will learn:

- How to adjust the hair attributes for achieving certain hair styles;

- How to achieve realistic looking hair colliding with the head geometry;

- How to use Hair Systems to create curtain effects;

- How to use hair to create sea creatures.

Braided hair

CREATING HAIR

Hair can be created on both NURBS and polygonal surfaces. Before you create the Hair System you should decide which renderer you will be using as this will affect the type of output you select.

You can render hair as Paint Effects™ strokes or you can convert the Paint Effects strokes to polygons and use another renderer such as mental ray. When you create hair, the visible result in the modeling view is the Hair System output.

Hair can be created in the form of NURBS curves (you would use this option if you want to use the Hair System for non-hair type simulations), Paint Effects strokes, or both curves and strokes.

There are three sets of curves for Hair Systems:

Start Position curves: This is the position of the hair at the start frame of a hair simulation. At creation time, these curves stick out straight from the follicles on the surface.

Rest Position curves: This is the position of the hair when no forces are affecting it. The shape of these curves can be edited to influence the look of the hair.

Current Position curves: These curves are reflecting how the hair behaves when you play the simulation.

You can choose to display any of the above mentioned curves while you set up your simulation from the **Hair** → **Display** menu.

Note:	Do not edit the Current Position curves as this will result in unpredictable results.

1 Steps to create hair

- Select the surface on which you want to create hair.
- From the Dynamics menu set, select **Hair** → **Create Hair** - ❑.
- Choose the desired options, then click on the **Create Hairs** button.

Note:	For polygons, UV's should fit between 0 and 1 and not be overlapping. You can use Automatic Mapping to quickly achieve this.

General steps for hair simulations

In order to create and animate hair for your models, in most cases you will go through the following general steps:

- Add hair to your models (see the steps outlined in the previous paragraph).

- Style the Hair Curves. This can be achieved by setting the Rest Position for the curves (based on the start position) and then editing the shape of the Rest Position curves.

- Change the hair dynamic behavior. This step will be outlined in the following paragraph.

- Set up the Hair Shading and Shadowing.

- Render the scene.

All the above mentioned steps will be further detailed through the exercises included in this chapter.

Modifying the hair dynamic behavior

You can use the Paint Hair Tool to modify the various attributes of the Hair System or the follicles, or you can use the Attribute Editor window to manually change the values for those attributes. In order to be able to tweak the hair attributes, you will need to select either the Hair System, hair follicles, or the Dynamic Curves.

1 To select the Hair System

- Select the *hairSystem* node in either the Outliner window or the Hypergraph window.

2 To select all the follicles in a Hair System

- In the Outliner window, select *hairSystemFollicles*.

- Select **Edit → Select Hierarchy**.

- **Ctrl-click** *hairSystemFollicles* to deselect it.

3 To select individual follicles

- In the Outliner window, click on the plus sign beside the *HairSystemFollicles* group node to expand it.

- Select the follicle you want to modify.

Note: You can also select the desired follicle in the Perspective view by clicking on the small circle at the base of the Hair Curve. You may find it easier to select follicles if you dolly in close to the surface and hide the Paint Effects Strokes.

Note: After you modify the Hair System or the follicle attributes, you may have to play the simulation in order to see the changes.

Interacting with the hair simulation

In the following steps, you will learn how to interactively Move, Scale, or Rotate the surface with hair while the simulation is playing, as well as see the hair update due to the dynamic forces applied to it.

1 Interacting with the hair simulation

- Select **Hair** → **Display** → **Current Position**.

  This changes the Hair Curves display to the current Dynamic Curves, that are the ones that update when you play the simulation.

- Select the surface with hair.

- In the Dynamics menu set, select **Solvers** → **Interactive Playback**. This will play the hair simulation, allowing you to interact with it at the same time.

- Select the **Move Tool** and move the surface with hair to see how the hair will behave due to the dynamic forces.

- Now select the **Scale** or **Rotate Tool** and manipulate the surface with hair to see how the hair behaves due to the dynamic forces.

Making the hair collide

In order for hair to interact with a surface, you must set the surface to collide with the hair before you play the simulation. Both polygonal geometry and NURBS surfaces can collide with hair. You can also make the hair collide with the ground, itself, or both.

1 Make the hair collide with a surface

- In the Outliner window (**Window** → **Outliner**), select the *hairSystem* node.

- **Shift-select** the geometry that you want to collide with the hair.

- In the Dynamics menu set, select **Hair** → **Make Collide**.

2 Make the hair collide with the ground and/or itself
- In the Outliner window, select the *hairSystem* node.
- Open the Attribute Editor (**Window** → **Attribute Editor**) for the *hairSystem*.
- Open the **Collisions** section in the Attribute Editor for the *hairSystem,* and turn on **Collide Ground**.
- Turn on **Self Collide** in the same section of the Attribute Editor for the *hairSystem.*

Setting up Hair Shadowing

Adding shadows to the hair will make it look more realistic. In order to achieve this effect, we will use a light with Depth map shadows set to **On**.

1 Set up hair self-shadowing
- Create a spot light and rotate it so it is pointing at the hair.
- In the light's Attribute Editor, open the **Shadows** section.
- Turn on **Use Depth Map Shadows**.
- Turn off **Use Mid Dist Dmap**.
- Optionally, turn **Off** the **Use Dmap Auto Focus** (to get better quality shadows), and then manually set the **Dmap Focus**.
- Increase the **Dmap Filter Size** to get softer shadows.
- Set the **Dmap Bias** to **0.006** or higher. This sets how far the light filters through the hair.
- In the Attribute Editor for the *hairSystem* node, open the **Shading** section and make sure that **Cast Shadows** is set to **On**.
- Render your scene to see the results.

Rendering hair

If you choose Paint Effects as the hair output (or Paint Effects and NURBS curves) when you create hair, you can then render it with the Maya Software Renderer. In order to render the hair using mental ray®, you have to first convert the Paint Effects strokes to polygons (**Modify** → **Convert** → **Paint Effects To Polygons**). You can also output just curves to another renderer, such as RenderMan®.

Tip:	You can render more hairs with fewer Paint Effects strokes by using Paint Effects Multi Streaks. These attributes are found in the Attribute Editor for the *hairSystemShape* node under the **Multi Streaks** section.

For more realistic results, turn on the Oversample and Oversample Post Filter options found in the Render Globals under the Paint Effects Rendering Options section.

CREATING DYNAMIC EFFECTS WITH HAIR

Within this section we will look at different ways of using Hair Systems for dynamic effects, such as curtains and underwater creatures. These types of effects are based on the dynamics of the Hair System, so we will output the hair as NURBS curves at creation time. The Dynamic Curves belonging to the Hair System can be used either as deformers for geometry or as lofting profiles as shown in the following exercise.

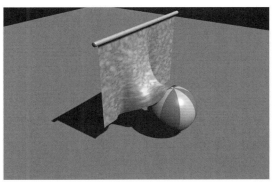

Curtain effect using Hair Curves as lofting profiles

Creating a curtain effect with hair

The next exercise will use a Hair System to generate the effect of a curtain that can interact with either the existing geometry, or with fields and forces (e.g. the density of a fluid container). The Hair System will use NURBS curves as output and the Current Position curves will be used as lofting profiles for the curtain surface. The higher the U and V count and the points per hair when we create the Hair System, the more accurate the simulation will be.

1 Open Curtain_Start.mb

- From the scenes directory found on the DVD-ROM, open the file named *Curtain_Start.mb*.

2 Create the Hair System

- Select the *CurtainRod* geometry.
- In the Dynamics menu set, select **Hair → Create Hair - □**.
- In the **Create Hair** options window, set the following values:

  Output to **NURBS Curves;**

  U Count to **14;**

  V Count to **1;**

  Points Per Hair to **10;**

  Passive Fill to **0;**

  Length to **10;**

  Randomization to **0.000;**

  Equalize to **On**.

- Make sure the **Create Rest Curves** and **Edge Bounded** are set to **Off**.
- Click on **Create Hairs**.

3 Lock the length of the start curves

- In the Dynamics menu set, select **Hair → Display → Start Position**.
- In the Perspective view, select the Hair Curves.
- In the Dynamics menu set, select **Hair → Modify Curves → Lock Length**.

4 Create the curtain surface

- In the Dynamics menu set, select **Hair → Display → Current Position**.

  This changes the Hair Curves display to the current Dynamic Curves, which are the ones that update when you play the simulation.

- In the Perspective view select the Hair Curves in order starting from the left.
- In the Modeling menu set, select **Surfaces → Loft**.
- In the Channel Box, rename the new surface to *Curtain*.

5 Make the curtain and the ball collide

- In the Outliner, select the *hairSystem* node.
- Hold the **Shift** key and in the Perspective view select the *ball* geometry.

- In the Dynamics menu set, select **Hair** → **Make Collide**.

6 Adjust the Collision attributes

- In the Outliner, select the *hairSystem* node.
- In the Attribute Editor window for the *hairSystem* node, open the **Collisions** sub-section.
- Turn on **Self Collide**. This will make the curtain surface collide with itself.
- Set **Repulsion** to **0.600**.
- Set **Num Collide Neighbors** to **5**.

7 Adjust the hair Stiffness and Gravity

- In the Attribute Editor window for the *hairSystem* node, open the **Dynamics** sub-section.
- Set **Stiffness** to **0.120**.
- In the Attribute Editor window for the *hairSystem* node, open the **Stiffness Scale** sub-section.
- Set **Gravity** to **3.000**.

8 Increase the geoConnector tessellation factor

- Select the *ball* geometry
- In the Channel Box under the Inputs section, select *geoConnector1*.
- Set the **Tessellation Factor** to **600**.

  This improves the resolution of the collisions stand-in object.

9 Playback the simulation interactively

- Select **Hair** → **Display** → **Current Position**. This changes the Hair Curves display to the current Dynamic Curves, which are the ones that update when you playback the simulation.
- Set your playback range to **20000** in the timeline.
- Select the *CurtainRod* geometry.
- In the Dynamics menu set, select **Solvers** → **Interactive Playback**. This will play the hair simulation, allowing you to interact with it at the same time.
- Select the **Move Tool** and start moving the *CurtainRod* geometry over the ball so they collide with each other.

Tip: For better results and to avoid interpenetration between the curtain surface and the ball, you can use a slightly bigger sphere as the collision object (that can be hidden after you set up the collisions), parented to the *ball* geometry.

Tip: Alternatively, you can use the above steps to create a bids curtain effect.

Using Hair Systems to create an octopus

During the following exercise, you will be using Hair Systems to create an octopus. The hair output will be set to NURBS curves at creation time and Paint Effects strokes will later be attached to these curves. The Paint Effects strokes will then be converted to Polygons, creating the octopus tentacles. The Hair Systems will be made to collide with the ground, and you can also make them collide with the other geometry in the scene.

Octopus using Hair Systems for dynamic behavior

1 Open Octopus_Start.mb

- Open the file named *Octopus_Start.mb*.

2 Creating the Hair Curves for tentacles

- From the **Create** menu, select **NURBS Primitives** → **Sphere**.

- Select *nurbsSphere1* and in the Dynamics menu set select **Hair** → **Create Hair** - ❐.

- In the **Create Hair** options window, set the following values:

  Output to **NURBS Curves**;

  U Count to **1**;

  V Count to **8**;

  Points Per Hair to **10**;

  Length to **5**.

- Click on **Create Hairs**.

3   Bring the tentacle.mel and octoBody.mel brushes onto the shelf

- Open the Script Editor window (**Window → General Editors → Script Editor**).

- In the Script Editor select **Edit → Clear All**.

- In the Script Editor select **File → Open Script**....

- Locate the *tentacle.mel* brush in the Brushes folder found on the Support Files DVD-ROM.

- Select the entire content of the input section from the Script Editor window, (**Ctrl+a**) and with the **MMB** drag it onto the shelf.

- In the Script Editor select **File → Open Script**...

- Open the *octoBody.mel* brush in the Brushes folder from the support files directory.

- Select the entire content of the input section from the Script Editor window (**Ctrl+a**), and with the **MMB**, drag it onto the shelf.

4   Create the tentacles and convert them to polygons

- Click on the first MEL™ button you created (*tentacle.mel*).

- In the Outliner window, expand the *hairSystem1OutputCurves* and **Shift-select** all the curves listed below it.

- In the Rendering menu set, select **Paint Effects → Curve Utilities → Attach Brush to Curves**. Paint Effects strokes will be generated along the Hair Curves.

- In the Outliner window, **Shift-select** all the strokes.

- In the **Modify** menu, select **Convert → Paint Effects to Polygons**.

  This will convert all the selected strokes into poly geometry.

5   Create the Hair System for the octopus body

- In the Outliner window select *nurbsSphere1* and in the Dynamics menu set select **Hair → Create Hair - ❑**.

- In the **Create Hair** options window, set the following values:

    Output to **NURBS Curves**;

    U Count to **1**;

    V Count to **1**;

    Points Per Hair to **5**;

    Length to **2**.

- Click on **Create Hairs**.

    This creates the second Hair System for the body.

6 Move the body hair follicle on top of the sphere

- In the Outliner window, expand the *hairSystem2Follicles* and select *nurbsSphere1Follicle*.

- Open the Attribute Editor window for the hair follicle, and in the **Follicle Attributes** section set the following values:

    Parameter U to **0.999**;

    Parameter V to **0.500**.

    This will move the NURBS curve of the second Hair System on top of *nurbsSphere1*.

7 Create the octopus body

- Click on the second MEL button you created (*octoBody.mel*).

- In the Outliner window, expand the *hairSystem2OutputCurves* and select the curve.

- In the Rendering menu set, select **Paint Effects → Curve Utilities → Attach Brush to Curves**.

    A Paint Effects stroke will be generated along the Hair Curve.

- In the Outliner window select the resulting stroke.

- In the **Modify** menu, select **Convert → Paint Effects to Polygons**.

    This will convert the selected stroke into poly geometry.

- In the Outliner window expand the *hairSystem2OutputCurves* and select the curve again.

- Using the **Move Tool**, move the octopus body until the bottom portion covers the tentacles.

8 Assign the octoBlinn shader to the octopus geometry

- Open the Hypershade window.

- In the Outliner, **Shift-select** all the *tentacleMeshGroup* nodes and then **Ctrl-select** the *octoBodyMeshGroup* node.

- **RMB** on the *octoBlinn* shader and choose **Assign Material to Selection** from the pop-up window.

9 Adjust the dynamic attributes for the tentacle Hair System

- In the Outliner window select *hairSystem1*.

- Open the Attribute Editor window for *hairSystem1* and in the Dynamics section set **Stiffness** to **0.165**.

- In the **Stiffness Scale** sub-section of the Dynamics section, set the following values:

    Damp to **0.083**;

    Friction to **0.555**;

    Gravity to **0.900**.

10 Make the tentacles collide with the ground

- In the Outliner window, select *hairSystem1*.

- Open the Attribute Editor window for *hairSystem1* and in the **Collisions** section set the following:

    Collide to **On**;

    Self Collide to **On**;

    Collide Ground to **On**.

11 Add turbulence to the tentacle motion

- In the Outliner window, select *hairSystem1*.

- Open the Attribute Editor window for *hairSystem1* and in the **Turbulence** section set the following:

    Intensity to **0.100**;

    Frequency to **0.777**;

    Speed to **0.661**.

12 Adjust the shape of the tentacle hair rest curves

- In the Outliner window, select *hairSystem1*.

- In the Dynamics menu set, select **Hair** → **Display** → **Start Position**. This will display the Start Position curves.

- In the Outliner window, expand the *hairSystem1Follicles* and **Shift-select** all the *nurbsSphereFollicle* nodes. This will select all the Start Position curves.

- In the Dynamics menu set, select **Hair** → **Set Rest Position** → **From Start**. This will create Rest Position curves.

- In the Perspective window, select **Show** → **Polygons**.

    This will hide the tentacle geometry, so that you can select the rest curves components.

- In the Dynamics menu set select **Hair** → **Display** → **Rest Position**. This will display the Rest Position curves.

- Change the selection mode from object to component and select all the CV's belonging to the Rest Position curves.

- In the Dynamics menu set select **Hair** → **Modify Curves** → **Curl** - ❐.

- In the options window, set the following values:

    Curl Amount to **0.500**;

    Curl Frequency to **0.300**.

- Click on **Curl Curves**.

13 Adjust the dynamic attributes for the body Hair System

- In the Outliner window, select *hairSystem2*.

- Open the Attribute Editor window for *hairSystem2* and in the Dynamics section set **Stiffness** to **1.000**.

- In the **Stiffness Scale** sub-section of the **Dynamics** section, set the following values:

    Damp to **0.050**;

    Friction to **1.000**;

    Gravity to **0.1**.

14 Add collisions to the octopus body

- In the Outliner window, select *hairSystem2*.

- Open the Attribute Editor window for *hairSystem2*, and in the **Collisions** section set the following:

    Collide to **On**;

    Self Collide to **On**;

    Collide Ground to **On**.

15 Playback the simulation interactively

- Select **Hair** → **Display** → **Current Position**.

This changes the Hair Curves display to the current Dynamic Curves, which are the ones that update when you play the simulation.

- Set your playback range to **20000** in the timeline.

- Select the *nurbsSphere1* geometry.

- In the Dynamics menu set select **Solvers → Interactive Playback**. This will play the hair simulation, allowing you to interact with it at the same time.

- Select the **Move Tool** and start moving the *nurbsSphere1* geometry around the objects in the scene.

  If you want to make the octopus collide with any of the objects in the scene, select the *hairSystem1* node and the object and in the Hair menu choose **Make Collide**. Then when you move the octopus above the objects you will see the tentacles collide with that object.

CREATING HUMAN HAIR

In this lesson, you will learn how to create two Hair Systems. The first Hair System will be made up of several hair clumps and bunched into position to create one large clump of hair.

The second Hair System will be created using one hair clump and will be positioned to stem from the first Hair System in the form of a ponytail.

You will also create a dynamic Newton field to influence the hair into position. In addition, a Hair Constraint will be applied to gather the hair clumps into position.

Creating a Hair System

A Hair System consists of the following elements: the *hairSystem*, *hairSystemFollicle*, and a specified *hairSystem* output. The *HairSystem* is the collection of the *HairSystemFollicles*. The *hairSystemFollicles* controls the attributes and curves associated with particular hair clump. Each follicle contains one NURBS curve that represents the position of the hair in that follicle.

The following is a scene of a girls head. Two display layers have been created to separate the skull sections and the facial, neck, and ear surfaces.

1 Create Hair System

Create a Hair System with the following options:

- Open the scene called *Sienna.mb.*

- In the Outliner, expand the node called *HeadQuadrants*.
- Select *Quadrant1*.

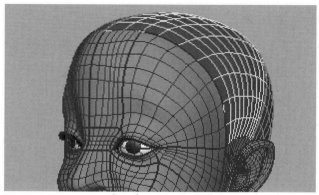

Quadrant1 selected

- Select **Hair** → **Create Hair** - ❏

    Output to **Paint Effects**;

    U Count to **10**;

    V Count to **10**;

    Points Per Hair to **10**;

    Passive Fill to **0**;

    Length to **15**;

    Randomization to **0**;

    Create Rest Curves to **Off**;

    Edge Bounded to **On**;

    Equalize to **On**.

- Click **Create Hairs**.

Tip: In the lesson we will keep the U and V Count to 10. This count allows for faster performance during playback of the dynamic simulation. However, for the effect of more full and thick hair, increase the U and V Count.

Hair System created

- Select **Hair** → **Display** → **Current and Start**.

  The hair follicles control the attributes and curves associated with each Paint Effects Hair Clump. The input to each follicle is a Start Position NURBS curve. Each follicle is attached to the *Quadrant1* surface at a specific UV position.

  The output of this *hairSystem* is in the form of Paint Effects curves. It can also be in the form of NURBS curves or both Paint Effects and NURBS curves.

Start hairs selected

- In the Outliner, select **Display** → **Shapes**.
- Select the *hairSystem1Follicles* node and expand.
- Select all the *Quadrant1Follicle* nodes within *hairSystem1Follicles* top node.

- In the Channel Box, set **Start Direction** to **Surface Normal**.

  The hairs will bend to follow the surface direction rather than the UV points on the surface.

- In the Attribute Editor, expand the **Clumps and Hair Shape** section. Set **Hairs Per Clump** to **5**.

  Hairs Per Clump is the number of hairs rendered for each Current Position Hair Curve. Since we are not rendering the hair at this point in the lesson, it is a good idea to decrease the amount of detail for each hair clump for faster performance during playback.

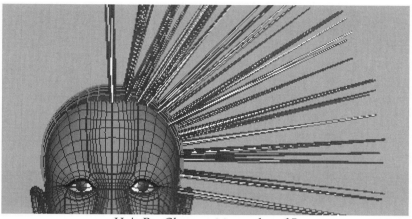

Hair Per Clump set to a value of 5

- **Playback** the scene.

  The hairs fall down due to the built-in force in the Y-direction simulating gravity.

2 Attach a Newton field to hairSystem1

A dynamic Newton field will be used to pull the hairs to a specific world location.

- Set playback end time in the **Range Slider** to end at frame **5000**.

- In the Outliner, select *hairSystem1* and select **Fields → Newton**.

  A dynamic Newton field is now connected to *hairSystem1*.

Note: In the Display Layer Editor, set the FaceSurfaces layer to Template in order to see the Newton field.

- In the Outliner, select *newtonField1.* In the Attribute Editor, set the following attribute values:

    Translate X to **20**;

    Translate Y to **20**;

    Magnitude to **350**;

    Attenuation to **0**.

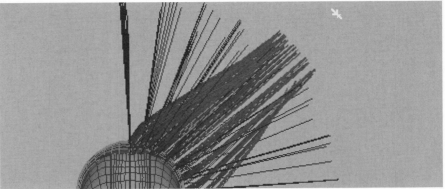

Current hairs are pulled towards the Newton field

- Playback until hairs fall into a relaxed position as they are pulled by the Newton field.
- Stop playback at frame **200**.
- In the Outliner, select the *HairSystem1.* In the Attribute Editor, under the **Dynamics** section, set **Stiffness** to a value of **0.050.**

3 Set the Current Position of hairs to the Start Position

- Select **Hair** → **Display** → **Current Position**.

Note: The Current Position can also be referred to as the *dynamic* position. For this reason, it is important to note that hairs must always be modified in the start or Rest Positions.

- In the Outliner, select the *pfxHair1* node (Current Position Hairs).
- Select **Hair** → **Set Start Position** → **From Current**.

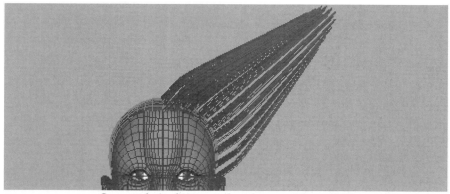
Current hairs become relaxed around frame 100

This ensures the Start Position hairs will assume the position of the current hairs when the simulation is rewound to the start frame.

- In the Outliner, select the *pfxHair1* node and select **Hair** → **Display** → **Start Position**.

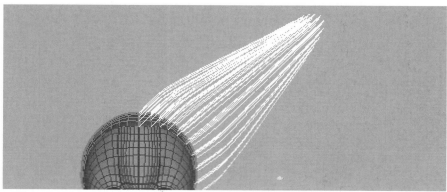
Start Position equals Current Position Hairs

4 Create a second Newton field

- Select the *hairSystem1* node and select **Fields** → **Newton**.

- In the Outliner, select *NewtonField2*. Open the Attribute Editor and set the following attribute values:

    Translate X to **8**;

    Translate Y to **8**;

    Magnitude to **250**;

    Attenuation to **0**.

- **Playback** the scene.

  Notice that the hairs are not affected by the dynamic fields. Start Hairs are displayed instead of the dynamic Current Hairs.

- Select **Hair** → **Display** → **Current Position**.

- **Playback** the scene until hairs become relaxed.

- **Stop** playback between frame **90-100**.

NewtonField2 afftecting Current Hairs

- In the Outliner, select *pfxHair1* and select **Hair** → **Set Start Position** → **From Current**.

- Select **Hair** → **Display** → **Start Position**.

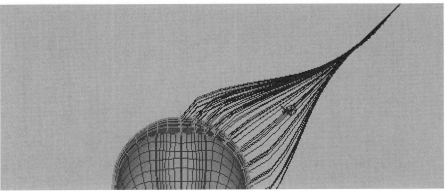

Start Position curves displayed

5 Delete End CV's of Start Position curves

- Select and drag the **Start Position curves** in the interactive view.

- Select **Hair** → **Convert Selection** → **to Start Curve End Cvs**.

Note: If the Hair System and Newton fields icon highlight in the process of your selection, Maya will still display the end CV's of the start curves.

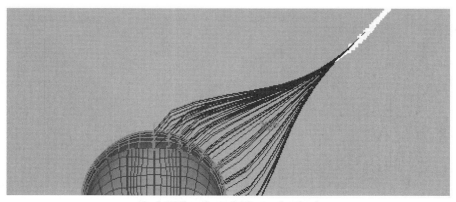

End CV's selected (first selection)

- Select **Edit** → **Delete**.

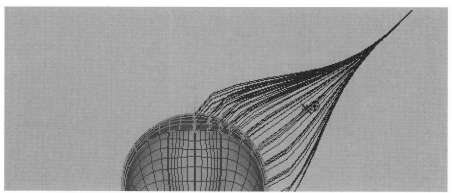

End CV's deleted

- In the interactive view, select the **Start Position curves** once again.
- Select **Hair** → **Convert Selection** → **to Start Curve End Cvs**.
- Select **Edit** → **Delete**.
- Repeat the above steps two more times.

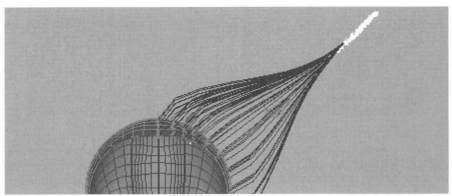

Start curves selected (second selection)

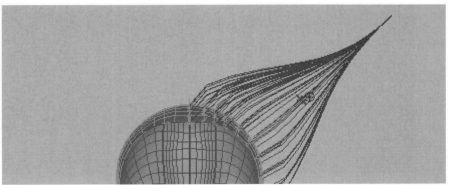

Start Curve end CV's deleted

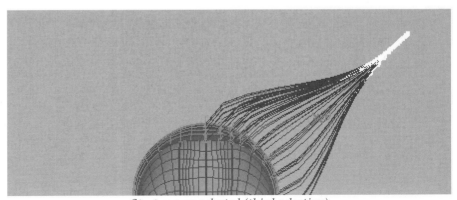

Start curves selected (third selection)

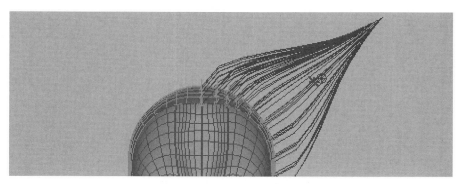

Start curve end CV's deleted

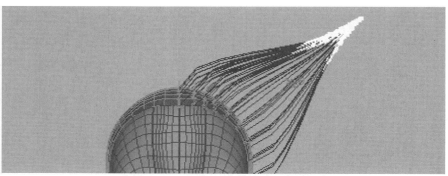

Start curves selected (fourth selection)

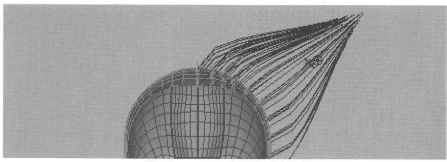

Start curves end CV's deleted

6 Modify Translation and Magnitude of NewtonField2

- In the Outliner, select *NewtonField2*.

- In the Channel Box, set the following attribute values:

    Translate X to **7**;

    Translate Y to **7**;

    Magnitude to **300**.

- Select **Hair** → **Display** → **Current Position**.

- In the Outliner, select *hairSystem1*.

- In the **Attribute Editor,** select the *hairSystemShape1* tab**.**
  Under Dynamics section, set **Stiffness** to **0.050.**

- **Playback** until hairs become relaxed (frame 100).

    As the hairs are pulled towards *NewtonField2*, they gather at the end points.

Hair pulled toward NewtonField2

- In the interactive view, select **Current Hairs.**

Note: For easier selection of Current Hairs, select the *pfxHair1* node in the Outliner.

- Select **Hair** → **Set Start Position** → **From Current.**
- Select **Hair** → **Display** → **Start Position.**

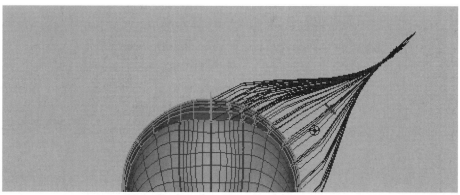

Hair displayed as Start Position curves

7 Create a Hair Constraint

A transform Hair Constraint will be used to Transform and Scale the hairs in closer to the *Quadrant1* surface.

- In the Outliner, select **Display → Shapes**.
- In the Outliner, select the *hairSystem1Follicles* node and expand.
- Select all follicles within the *hairSystem1Follicles* top node.

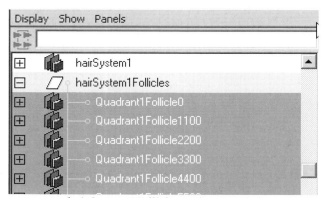

hairSystem1Follicles node expanded

Note: It is better to select all the *hairSystem1Follicles* in the Outliner to ensure all follicles are selected.

- Select **Hair → Create Constraint → Transform**.
- In the Outliner, select the *hairConstraint1* node and expand.

- In the Attribute Editor, select the *hairConstraint1* tab.
- Set the following values for Start Position of the hair Transform Constraint:

    Translate X to **5.2**;

    Translate Y to **6.4**.

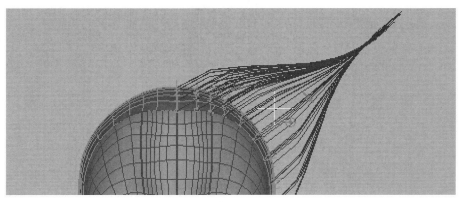

8 Interacting with the hair simulation

In these next steps we will interact with the playback of the hair simulation by Translating and Scaling the Transform Constraint to pull the hair into a bunched position.

- Set the Time Slider to frame **1**.
- Select **Hair → Display → Current Position**.
- Select **Solvers → Interactive Playback**.
- With the Hair Constraint selected, **Translate** and **Scale** the Transform Constraint into position.

Note: Scale the Transform Constraint first, then translate.

- Stop playback when the hairs are neatly collected closer to the surface.
- In the Outliner, select the *pfxHair1* node.

- Select **Hair** → **Set Start Position** → **From Current**.

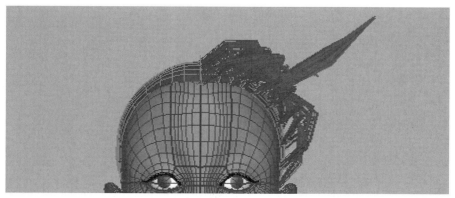

Transform Constraint, translated and scaled into position

Note: The end result of the hair appearance and position will vary.

9 Edit the translate and scale values of the hair Transform Constraint (optional)

After playback, you can further modify the Transform Constraint Translate and Scale values if you are not yet satisfied with the position of Transform Hair Constraint.

- In the Outliner, select the *hairConstraint1* node.
- In the Attribute Editor, select the *hairConstraint1* tab and set the following:

    Translate X to **5.0**;

    Translate Y to **6.0**;

    Translate Z to **0.328**;

    Scale X to **0.30**;

    Scale Y to **0.30**;

    Scale Z to **0.30**.

After the translate and scale values have been changed for the hair Transform Constraint, do the following:

- **Playback** the simulation until the hairs become rested.
- **Stop** playback.

- In the interactive view, select the **Current Hairs** or the *pfxHair1* node in the Outliner.
- Select **Hair** → **Set Start Position** → **From Current**.

10 Adjust the Damping of hairs

Damp simulates friction with air. However, in this example, we will increase the damp value to give the hair more stability. The higher the damp value, the less inertial motion on the Current Position hairs.

In the Outliner, select the *hairSystem1* node and open the Attribute Editor.

- Open the **Dynamics** section.
- Under the **Stiffness Scale** section, set **Damp** to **0.2**.
- Playback the hairs until they become relaxed.
- In the Outliner, select the *pfxHair1* node.
- Select **Hair** → **Set Start Position** → **From Current**.

Current Hair Damp value set to 0.2

11 Cut Start Position hairs

- Select **Hair** → **Display** → **Start Position**.
- In the interactive view, zoom up and select the longest Start Position curves that stem outward from the gathering point.

- Select **Hair** → **Convert Select** → **to Start Curves and End Cvs**.

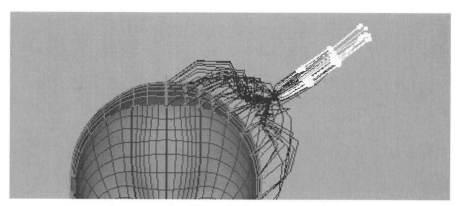

Longest ends of Start Position curves selected

- Select **Edit** → **Delete**.
- Repeat this process to clip the remaining hair ends.

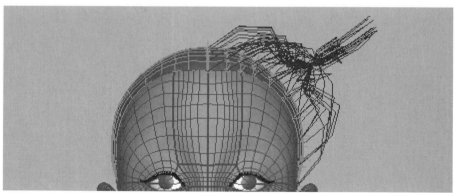

Longest ends of Start Position curves deleted

- In the interactive view, zoom in once again to select the second longest Start Position curves.

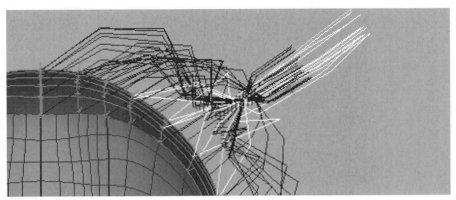

Second longest Start Position curves selected

- Select **Hair** → **Convert Select** → **to Start Curves and End Cvs**.

Second longest Start Position curve end CV's highlighted.

- Select **Edit** → **Delete**.

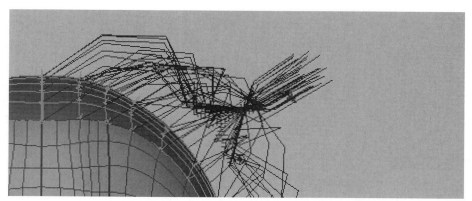

Second longest Start Position curve end CV's deleted

Repeat this process for the last group of end CV's for *hairSystem1*.

- Zoom in and select the third group of long ends.
- Select **Hair** → **Convert Select** → **to Start Curves and End Cvs**.

Third longest Start Position curve end CV's highlighted

- Select **Edit** → **Delete**.

Third longest Start Position curve end CV's deleted

Creating a ponytail

In this next section, we will create a second Hair System that will stem from the first Hair System in the form of a ponytail.

1 Create a second Hair System

- Open the scene called *Sienna0.mb*.
- In the Outliner, select *hairSystem1Follicles*.
- Select **Hair** → **Display** → **Start Position**.
- In the Outliner, expand the *HeadQuadrants* group node and select *Quadrant1*.

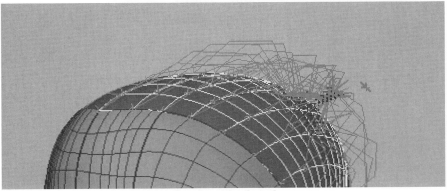

Quadrant1 selected

- Select **Hair** → **Create Hair** → **Options**.

- Set the following:

    Output to **Paint Effects and Nurbs Curve**;

    U Count to **1**;

    V Count to **1**;

    Points Per Hair to **10**;

    Passive Fill to **0**;

    Length to **20**;

    Randomization to **0**;

    Create Rest Curves to **Off**;

    Edge Bounded to **Off**;

    Equalize to **Off**;

    Select **Create Hairs**.

Note: Points Per Hair is the number of points/segments per hair. Increase this value for a smoother curve during the hair simulations.

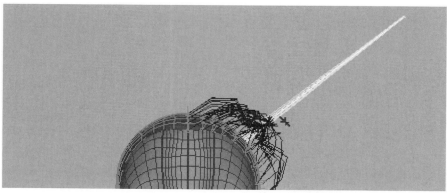

Second Hair System (hairSystem2) created

- **Playback** the scene to see the effect of gravity on the single hair follicle.

2 Modify UV Parameter of the hairSystem2Follicles

- In the Outliner, select the *hairSystem2Follicles* node and expand.
- Select *Quadrant1Follicle5050*.

- In the Attribute Editor, set the following values for Parameter U and V:

  Parameter U to **0.605**;

  Parameter V to **0.532**.

Note: The *hairSystem2Follicles* parameter U and V values will vary depending on where the gathering point of hairSystem1 is located.

Parameter U and V set for hairSystem2

3 Move CV's on the hairSystem2 Follicle

- In the Outliner, select the *hairSystem2* node.
- Select **Hair** → **Display** → **Start Position**.

Start Curve displayed for hairSystem2

- With the Start Position curve selected, select **Display → NURBS Components → CVs**.

- Go to component mode.

- **Double-click** on the **Move Tool** to open the options box.

- In the **Move Settings** section, set **Move** to **Local**.

  This will ensure that the movement is constrained to the axes in the local space coordinate system, rather than the world space coordinate system.

- In the Top view, move the second CV on the Z-axis along the curve. The second CV should sit above the end points of the *hairSystem1* start curves.

- Move the third and fourth CV's so that they are evenly placed along the curve.

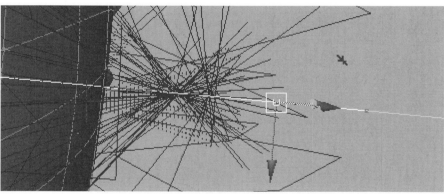

First CV moved to the end points of hairSystem1 start curves

- With *hairSystemFollicle2* still selected, select **Hair → Display → Current Position**.

- **Playback** the scene.

  The hair will flex at the point where the second CV is positioned.

- **Stop** playback.

Flex starts at second CV

4 Modify the hairSystem2Follicles attribute

- In the Outliner, select the *hairSystem2Follicles* node and expand.
- Select the *Quadrant1Follicle5050* and open the Attribute Editor.
- Select the Quadrand1FollicleShape5050 tab.
- Under Follicle Attributes set the following:

  set **Degree** to **3**;

  set **Braid** to **On**.

- Under Dynamic Overrides set the following:

  check **Override Dynamics** to **On**;

  set **Stiffness** to **0.550**.

5 Modify the hairSystem2 node attributes

- In the Outliner, select the *hairSystem2* node.
- In the Attribute Editor, select the hairSystemShape2 tab and set the following:

  Display Quality to **100**.

  This value is the percentage of hairs within clumps (Paint Effect Strokes) to display for interactive draw. By decreasing the default value of 100 to 50, we are increasing performance during playback.

- Under Clump and Hair Shape, set the following:

  Hairs Per Clump to **150**;

  Sub Segments to **25**.

Hairs Per Clump is the number of hairs rendered for each Current Position Hair Curve. **Sub Segments** determines the number of smoothly interpolated segments at render time.

Clump Twist to **0.550**.

The **Clump Twist** rotates the clump around the primary hair axis.

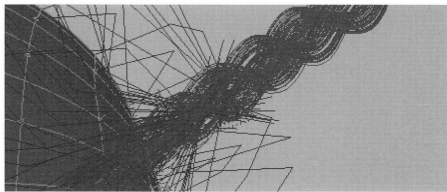

Clump Twist

Clump Width to **1.0**.

The **Clump Width** is the base or maximum width for each hair clump.

6 Set Clump Width Scale

Under Clump Width Scale there is a graph which can define a varied width for hair clumps. The left of the graph represents the width of the clump root. The right of the graph represents the width of the clump tip.

Modify your graph to match the illustration:

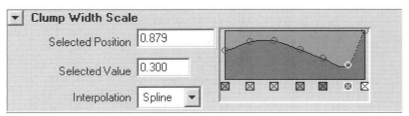

Clump Width Scale graph

Note: To add a marker, select anywhere along the line of the graph. To delete a marker, select the squares with the X at the bottom of the graph.

7 Add Thinning to the base hairs of the braid

- With *hairSystem2* Attribute Editor still open and the hairSystemShape2 tab open, under **Clump and Hair Shape**, set **Thinning** to a value of **0.256**.

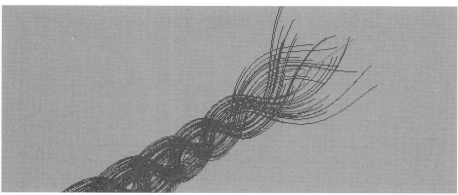

Thinning applied to the base of the braid

8 Adjust Dynamic and Stiffness Scale attributes

Additional gravity will be applied to the braid and more stiffness will be increased between the base of the braid and the intersection point where the braid meets with the hair end points of *hairSystem1*.

- In the Outliner, select *hairSystem2*.

- In the Attribute Editor, select the hairSystemShape2 tab.

- Under **Dynamics**, increase **Stiffness** to **0.800**.

  Stiffness is the amount the hair can flex (bend).

- Set the Stiffness Scale graph as shown by the illustration below:

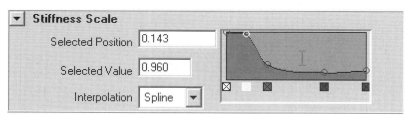

Stiffness Scale graph

In the above graph, the first two markers are set to a Stiffness Scale value of 1 so that the braid will remain stiff from the base to point where the braid intersects with the hair end points of the *hairSystem1*.

The third and fourth marker values are less than a value of 1, which will allow more flex in the braid at the middle and end regions.

Stiffness Scale affects the stiffness from the root to the tip of the braid. The left of the graph represents Stiffness at the root of the braid and the right of the graph represents the Stiffness at the tip of the braid.

The Stiffness Scale attributes multiplies the Stiffness attribute. A value of 1.0 will leave Stiffness unchanged, but if the value is 0, the Stiffness Scale attribute will have no effect.

Note: Click on the line representing the graph to create a marker. Click on the box with the X to delete a marker.

- Set **Drag** to **0.050;**
- Set **Damp** to **0.200;**
- Set **Gravity** to **10.0**.
- **Playback** the simulation until the hair becomes relaxed (approx. frame 200-210).
- **Stop** playback.

Tip: Decrease the value for Display Quality of *hairStystem2* for faster interactive playback.

- In the Outliner, select *pfxHair2*.
- Select **Hair → Set Start Position → From Current**.

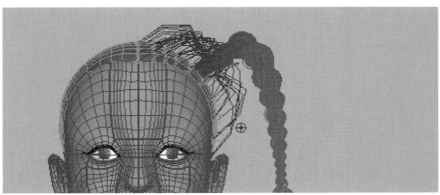

HairSystem2 relaxed

9 Modifying hair attributes for hairSystem1

- In the Outliner, select *pfxHair1*.

- Select **Hair** → **Display** → **Current Position**.
- In the Outliner, select *hairSystem1* node.
- In the Attribute Editor select the hairSystemShape1 tab.
- Set **Display Quality** to **100**.
- Under **Clump and Hair Shape**, set the following:

  Hair Per Clump to **180**;

  Sub Segments to **20**;

  Clump Width to **0.800**.

Hairsystem1 modified

Note: For faster interactive previews while tweaking, decrease the attribute value for *Display Quality,* on the Hair System nodes.

- In the Outliner, select the *hairSystem1Follicles* node and expand.
- **Shift-select** all *Quadrant1Follicle* nodes with the *hairSystem1Follicles* group.
- In the Channel Box, set the following attributes:

  Clump Width Mult to **1.2**.

  The **Clump Width Mult** multiplies the global Hair Clump Width on *hairSystem1* node. If the Clump Width is a value of 0, the Clump Width Mult value has no effect. The Default value is 1.

  Density Mult to **1.5**.

The Density Mult multiplies the number of hairs relative to the global Hair Per Clump on the *hairSystem1* node. If the Hairs Per Clump on the *hairSystem1* is 0, then the Density Mult value has no effect. The Default value is 1.

Note: Increasing the Clump Width Mult and Density Mult may slow down rendering performance considerably. Decrease these values as necessary.

Tip: If the Hair Clumps appear to stick out from the surface (hairline), you can paint the Hair Inset Value using the **Paint Hair Tool**.

---

10 Modifying hair attributes for hairSystem2

- In the Outliner, select the *hairSystem2* node.
- In the Attribute Editor, select the hairSystemShape2 tab.
- Set **Display Quality** to **100**.
- Under **Clump and Hair Shape**, set the following:

  Hair Per Clump to **300**;

  Sub Segments to **40**;

  Clump Width to **1.5**.

- In the Outliner, select the *hairSystem2Follicles* node and expand.
- Select the *Quadrant1Follicle5050* node.
- In the Channel Box, set the following attributes:

  Clump Width Mult to **1.2**;

  Density Mult to **1.3**.

HairSystem2 modified

11 Set Shading for hairSystem1

- In the Outliner, select *hairSystem1* node.
- In the Attribute Editor, select the *hairSystemShape1* node.
- Scroll down to the Shading section.
- Click the **Hair Color** swatch to select a dark brown color from the Color Chooser window. Lower the horizontal manipulator to the bottom on the left vertical bar in the Color Chooser window.

- Set the following values:

  H to **40.0**;

  S to **0.500**;

  V to **0.060**.

- Render to see the hair color.

  To add some realism we will use the **Hair Color Scale** attribute to create variation in the hair color.

- With the *hairSystemShape1* node still selected in the Attribute Editor, expand the Hair Color Scale section.
- Set the graph to look like the following.

  The Hair Color Scale uses a ramp (gradient) to control and blend the colors of the hair. Click inside the ramp to create a marker. Click the box with an X to delete a marker. Select each circular handle above the ramp to select and modify each color entry.

The active color (middle color entry) will have a white border around the circle at the top of the ramp and a white border at the box below the ramp.

The color on the left side of the ramp represents the color at the root of the *hairSystem1*. The color on the right side of the ramp represents the color at the tip of *hairSystem1*.

- Delete the middle color entry locator.
- Select the first color entry locator on the left side of the graph.
- Select the **Selected Color** swatch.
- In the color chooser, set the following values:

    H to **40.0**;

    S to **1.0**;

    V to **0.070**.

- Set the **Selected Position** to **0.50**.

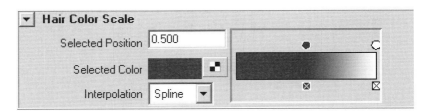

Hair Color Scale graph

- Set **Translucence** to **0.8**.
- Select the swatch next to **Specular Color**.
- In the **Color Chooser** window, set the following:

    H to **40.0**;

    S to **0**;

    V to **0.150**;

    Specular Power to **3.0**;

    Cast Shadows to **On**.

Translucence allows light to filter through for a softer effect. Specular Color is the input of color for specular highlights. Cast Shadows causes the hair to cast shadows (Depth Map) only.

12 Set Color Randomization for hairSystem1

Curly or coarse hair has many randomizations of color and highlights. For realism, we will set values for the following attributes that randomize hair color, brightness, and specular brightness of *hairSystem1*.

- Expand the **Color Randomization** and set the following attributes:

  Diffuse Rand to **0.8**;

  Specular Rand to **0.5**;

  Hue Rand to **0**;

  Sat Rand to **0**;

  Val Rand to **0.350**.

- Render to see results.

13 Add Displacements to hairSystem1

Curl is the amount of curl displacement applied to each hair. Curl Frequency influences the rate of the curl where larger values create more curl. Noise is the amount of Perlin Noise (preset texture) displacement of the hair. Noise Frequency is the spacial scale of the noise offset along the hair. Increasing this value results in finer, kinkier hair.

To make hair appear curly, we will adjust attributes to control the displacement properties of the hair.

- With *hairSystemShape1* tab selected in the Attribute Editor, open the **Displacement** section and set the following:

  Curl to **0.4**;

  Curl Frequency to **15**;

  Noise to **0.5**;

  Noise Frequency to **1.5**.

- Render to see results.
- Repeat Shading and Color Randomization settings to *hairSystem2*.

Note: Make sure that the Density Mult of both hairSystem1 and hairSystem2 match when rendered to keep density consistent throughout the hair body.

---

14 Add Displacements to hairSystem2

We will adjust the curl of *hairSystem2* to match the curl consistency of *hairSystem1*.

- Select the *hairSystem2* in the Outliner and open the Attribute Editor.

- Select the *hairSystemShape2* tab and expand the **Displacements** section. Set the following values:

  Curl to **0.8**;

  Curl Frequency to **20**;

  Noise to **0.5**;

  Noise Frequency to **1.5**.

- **Render** to see the results.

15 Set-up Shadows and Self Shadows for both hairSystems

- To create a point light select **Create → Lights → Point Light**.

- In the Outliner, select *pointLight1* and open the Attribute Editor.

- In the Attribute Editor, select the *pointLightShape1* tab.

- Under the **Point Light** attributes section, set:

  Intensity to **.20**.

- Hit the **7** key on your keyboard to show the illumination of the point light.

- Translate light until it points to *hairSystem1* and *hairSystem2*.

- In the Attribute Editor, for *pointLightShape1*, open the **Shadow** section and set the following:

  Use Depth Map Shadows to **On**;

  Use Mid Dist Dmap to **Off**;

  Use Dmap Auto Focus to **On** (optional);

  Dmap Filter Size to **2**.

  The Dmap Filter will blur the light on the hair for realism.

- **Dmap Bias** to **0.006 (or higher)**.

  The Dmap Bias sets how far the light filters through the hair.

16 Position a hair clip in place for both hairSystems

- In the Outliner, select the *hairSystem1* node.

- Select **Hair → Display → Start Position**.

- In the Outliner, select the *hairSystem2* node.

- Select **Hair → Display → Start Position**.

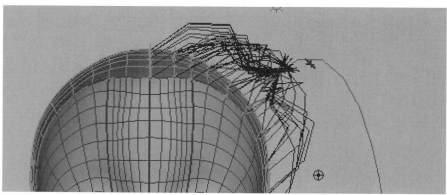

Start hairs displayed for hairSystem1 and hairSystem2

- In the Outliner, select *hairSystem2Follicles* node and expand.
- Select the *Quadrant1Follicle5050* within the *hairSystem2Follicles* parent node.
- Hit the **F8** key on your keyboard to switch to component mode.
- Select the second CV on the follicle curve.

Second CV on curve selected

- Hit **F2** on your keyboard to switch to the Animation menu set.
- Select **Deform** → **Create Cluster - ❑**.
- Set **Relative** to **Off**.
- Select **Create**.

Cluster created for the second CV on the start curve

- In the Layer Editor, make the layer called *HairAccessories* visible. The hair clip object sits at the origin.
- Change to Wireframe mode in order to see the hair clip object.
- In the Outliner select the *HairClip* node.
- Translate, Rotate, and Scale the hair clip to where both Hair Systems Start curves intersect.
- In the Outliner, using your **MMB**, to **drag+drop** the *cluster1Handle* node onto the *HairClip* node.

  The hair clip will be parented to *hairSystem2*.

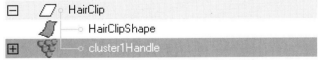

cluster1Handle parented to HairClip

- Select **F4** on your keyboard to switch back to the Dynamics menu set.
- Select **Hair** → **Display** → **Current Position**.
- Translate, Rotate, and Scale the *HairClip* object to cover the intersecting point of both Hair Systems in their current position.

Hair clip at the intersecting point of both Hair Systems

As necessary, modify the Clump Width Scale (graph) of hairSystem2, so the current position hairs do not go through the hair clip or adjust the Translate and Scale of the hair clip to compensate for the clump width of hairSystem2.

Note: As needed, increase the **Density Mult** of *hairSystem2Follicles* so that the hairs match the hair density of the *hairSystem1Follicles*.

17 Rendering the hair

You will now render the Paint Effects hair using the Maya Software Renderer.

- Select **Windows → Rendering Editors → Render Globals...**
- Select **Render Using → Maya Software** from the dropdown menu.
- Select the Maya Software tab.
- Scroll down and open the **Paint Effects Rendering Options** section.
- Set the following:

  Oversample to **On**;

  Oversample Post Filter to **On**.

  The **Oversample** and **Oversample Post Filter** options are useful when rendering Paint Effects hair.

  Oversample renders the Paint Effects at a double resolution for better anti-aliasing.

  Oversample Post Filter applies a weighted filter to the oversampled image for better smoothing.

- Render the current frame. **Render → Render Current Frame**.

Note: If you want to render frames, set your desired options for the **Image File Output** and **Resolution** sections of the Common tab in the Render Global Settings.

Conclusion

In this chapter you learned how to create dynamic effects with hair using NURBS curves. You used the Paint Hair Tool to modify the various attributes that belong to the Hair System, and make hair collide with a surface. You also learned how to work with two Hair Systems to create realistic human hair in a form of a ponytail. You then modified the Hair System and worked with a Hair Contraint to gather the clumps into one hair bunch. Finally, you used the Maya Software Renderer to render the hair.

In the next chapter, you will learn how to use Maya Cloth to create various cloth garments and run realistic cloth simulations.

4 Maya Cloth

This chapter teaches animators, modelers and effects artists how to plan and carry out cloth simulations at an intermediate level within the Maya environment. The focus will be on establishing sound workflow practices on a variety of effects to explore the relevant tools and their application.

Meet "Ichabod"

The cloth chapter will be explored with a character called *Ichabod*. Ichabod has been modeled, textured and character controls have been setup in Maya for you. This will allow you to focus on cloth and not have to worry about these other issues.

A number of garments will be created for Ichabod as the features of Maya Cloth are explored.

Outcomes

After successfully completing this chapter you will be able to:

- Create various garments;
- Tailor garments;
- Create other cloth objects like curtains;
- Run clothing simulations;
- Use constraints to adjust the behavior of the clothing;
- Transfer garments to different scenes;
- Make reusable cloth cache files.

Maya Cloth

Maya cloth is a spring based dynamics system that adds new simulation possibilities to Maya. The cloth solvers can be used with the existing dynamics solvers but do behave differently. It is much easier to simulate clothing and other flowing type objects with the cloth solver than it is with the traditional soft body dynamics that have been used in the past.

Cloth can be used to create obvious things like clothing and drapery as well as more natural objects such as flower petals.

Clothing is created with Maya Cloth much the same way as it is in real-life. Patterns are designed and then sewn together. Of course, modifying the pattern and the types of material used in the clothing is much easier and freer with Maya.

Properties like thickness, crease angle of seams, stretch and bend resistance all add to the power of cloth and the variety of simulations that can be created.

Installing the data

The directory *Cloth_data* on the included DVD-ROM contains all the data you need to use this product. This folder contains a number of subfolders, each with important elements that can be copied to your local drive. To install the data from the DVD-ROM, copy the *Cloth_data* directory into your *maya/projects/*directory.

Dataset list

Below is a breakdown of the subfolders within *Cloth_data*:

Scenes - Maya scene files (.mb) and cloth cache files that accompany the various lessons in the book.

Movies - Sample movies (.mpeg) of various cloth examples and playblasts of finished exercises.

PropertyMovies - Sample movies (.mpeg) of cloth with a variety of important property attribute settings. These are helpful for quickly visualizing what effect the various attributes have on cloth.

Textures - Contains texture files (.rgb) for the texturing lesson.

Images - Various still cloth images generated from the lessons.

Extras - Contains completed scene files from many of the lessons and some extra information pages and example files.

MAKING A ROBE

This lesson will introduce the basics of cloth. It will be a review of a simple piece of clothing. For this lesson you will be making a Grim Reaper type of robe for the character.

Create a robe

When creating the robe, you will learn the following:

- Create panels and seam them together to form garments;
- Relaxing and fitting a garment;
- Basic panel and solver attributes.

Making a robe

In this lesson you will make a Grim Reaper style robe for Ichabod. A robe is a fairly simple garment that will allow you to review concepts from the standard cloth tutorials and look at some advanced issues.

Making a garment can be broken down into a number of steps:

- Creating curves to define panels;
- Creating panels from curves;
- Sewing (or seaming) the panels together;

- Relaxing the garment on the character;
- Adjusting panel and solver properties.

Creating curves for the rear panels

Panels are the building blocks of any garment. Panels are defined by curves that make a closed shape. The panel curves must be coplanar, or, in other words, lie in a flat plane.

The main part of a robe is the back panel. It will be created first and the other panels will be built from it. The front of a garment is usually a more complicated version of the rear panels. Building the rear panels first, makes a good foundation for the clothing.

1 Open a file

- Select **File** → **Open**.
- Navigate to the *$HOME/maya/scenes* directory.
- Open the file called *01.IchabodCharacter*.

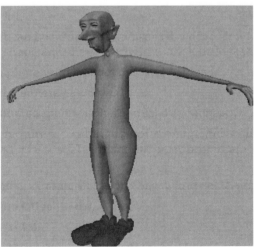

Ichabod ready for clothing

2 Template Ichabod

The geometry for Ichabod is located on the highRezLayer in the Layer Editor.

- Template the *highRezLayer* layer.

    Layers are used for organization. Cloth requires a fair amount of set-up and nodes. Using layers will help you to work quickly.

3 Change the grid settings

- To change the grid settings, select **Display** → **Grid** - ⊐, and set the following:

  Subdivisions to **10**.

  Panel curve end points must define a closed shape. Grid snapping helps to ensure that the shape will be closed.

4 Place curves to define a rear body panel

Work in the front view. This will ensure that the curves are coplanar. You will also need to ensure that all the edit points are touching each other.

- Place four edit point curves with **Create** → **EP Curve Tool** and use grid snapping to create a shape as shown below.

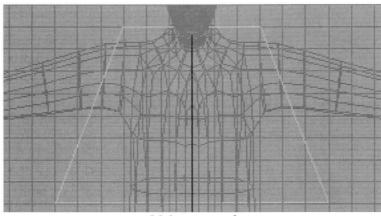

Main rear panel

5 Group the curves and rename them

- Select the new curves, and select **Edit** → **Group**.

- **Rename** the group node *topCurves*.

  Grouping the curve will help in organizing and selecting.

6 Duplicate and unparent the bottom curve

The bottom curve of the panel will be the top curve of the panel below. Duplicating curves can make panel creation and editing easier.

  The top panel can be hidden temporarily.

7 Create the bottom rear panel

- Add three more curves to define the bottom panel for the robe.

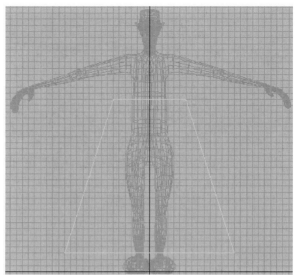

Bottom panel

8 Group the curves and rename them

- **Group** the curves.
- Rename the group node *bottomCurves*.

Note: Remember to include the curve that was duplicated from the top panel.

---

9 Duplicate and unparent the top curve of the main panel

The top curve of the main panel will be the bottom curve of the hood panel above. The top panel can be hidden temporarily.

10 Create the rear hood panel

- Add two more curves to define the hood panel for the robe.

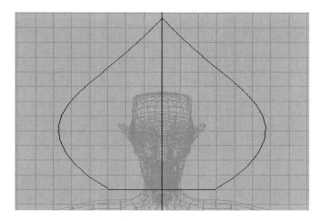

Create a panel for the hood

11 Group the curves and rename them

- Rename the group node *hoodCurves*.

Note: Remember to include the curve that was duplicated from the top panel.

---

12 Save your work

The rear panels for Ichabod's robe should now be created. The sleeves and front panels will be built from this.

Creating curves for the sleeve panels

Now that the body part of the robe has been created, the sleeves can be made. It is a good idea to create the sleeves as secondary objects built from the body.

1   Duplicate a side curve from the main back panel

2   Build three curves to make a panel

3   Group the curves

- Name the group of curves *sleeveCurves*.

4   Mirror the group to make the opposite sleeve

- Use the **Duplicate** tool with **Scale X** set to **-1.0**.

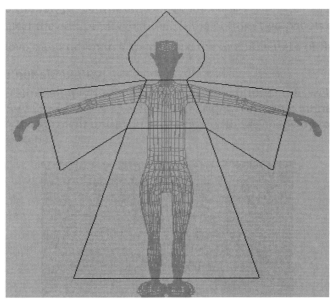

The robe with sleeves

5 Duplicate the sleeve panels and move them forward

You should now have four *sleeveCurves* groups.

6 Save your work

Create front panel curves

The front panels for a robe are not much more complicated than the rear panels. A robe can open like a jacket which will require more panels but this one will be a pull-over type. The hood will require an opening for Ichabod to see through.

1 Duplicate the rear panels

- **Duplicate** the hood, top and bottom panels.

  These copies will be modified to make the front panels for the robe.

2 Create a half length curve for the base of the hood panel

The front part of the hood must be created as two panels so that a face opening can be made. The best way to do this is by creating a right and a left half for the hood.

One half will be created and the other half will be mirrored across.

Hiding all of the curve groups but the front main panel and the hood may help to keep things clear.

- **Delete** the curve at the top of the main panel and at the base of the hood.

- Add curves as shown below.

  Each side of the hood should be composed of five curves.

3 Group the curves

- Name the group *hoodCurves*.

4 Mirror the group to make the opposite side of the hood

- Use the **Duplicate** tool with **Scale X** set to **-1.0**.

5 Duplicate the bottom hood curves for the main panel

- **Group** these curves into the *topCurves* node.

  This panel should now be composed of five curves.

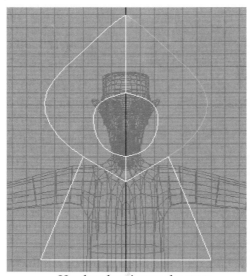

Hood and main panel curves

6 Save your work

All the panels required to make the robe should now be completed.

Aligning curves for panels

If you look at this Ichabod and the panels that have been created in the side view, you should see that they intersect his body. Panels should be created close to the model, but not intersecting.

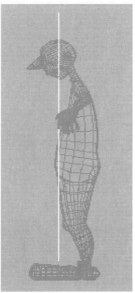

Panel curves need to be aligned

1 Move the panels backwards or forwards

- Select all the group nodes created above, and move them backwards or forwards.

  Some curve nodes should move more than others. For the back of the robe, the hood will move the least and the bottom will move the most. This is why curves that are common between panels were duplicated - it allows for more flexibility and precision when aligning panels. Each panel can be moved as much or as little as necessary without having to worry about a negative effect on other panels.

- Tweak any placement on individual curve nodes as you see fit.

  Remember that the curves should be close to Ichabod but not intersecting.

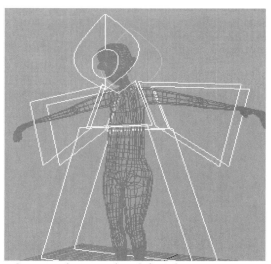
Curve nodes moved to define the garment

2 Rotate the hood panels

To get more precise garment creation, the panel curves can be rotated as well. Ichabod's head and neck are far forward from the rest of his body. Rotating the hood panels will improve the garment fitting. Remember to keep the curves planar.

- Select the *hoodCurve* nodes.

- Press the **e** key to go into rotate mode.

  Notice that the pivot point of the nodes are located near Ichabod's feet. The pivots should be moved to get better control of the rotation.

- Press the **Insert** key to enter pivot move mode.

- **Move** the pivots up to the base of the curves.

- Press **Insert** to return to rotate mode.

- **Rotate** the panels so that they align with Ichabod's head and neck.

- **Move** the front hood curves together so that they have the same alignment.

  This procedure can be repeated for any other curve nodes you like.

  After rotating the curve nodes, you may need to move them again to get a better alignment.

  The front curves can also be moved down a bit.

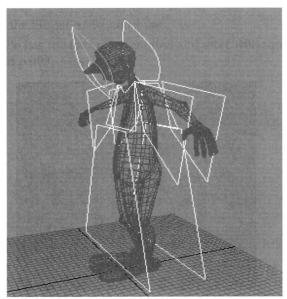

Final alignment of robe curves

3 Transfer all the curves to a new layer

Layers are useful to organize the scene. Cloth has many elements and organization is important.

4 Save your work

Ichabod should now be ready for the next step of creating panels.

Making panels

Now that all the curves have been built, panels can be created from them. Panels are the individual pieces of fabric that make up a garment.

1 Make the curves into panels

To make a panel, all the curves that define the closed shape must be selected. Since the curves that define each panel were grouped, each curve node can be selected and made into a panel very easily.

- Select a curve group node.

  For simplicity, nodes can be selected in the Hypergraph.

- Select **Cloth** → **Create Panel**.

Tip: It is good practice to name each panel after creating it.

2 Repeat step 1 until all the panels are defined

You should have one panel for each group of curves.

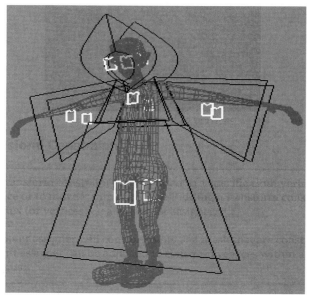

Panels created for the robe

3 Assign a property to the panels

- Select all the panels.

Tip: A useful MEL button to make for your shelf is:
```
select "panel*";
```

- Select **Simulation** → **Properties** → **Create Property**.

    Any panels that are selected when a property is created, will have the new property assigned to them.

- Rename the new property *robeProperty* in the Channel Box.

4 Adjust the cloth properties

- Set the following properties:

    U/V Bend Resistance to **60**;

    Shear Resistance to **60**;

    Density to **0.5**;

    Thickness to **3**;

    Thickness Force to **30**.

    Cloth properties will be looked at in greater detail in the following lessons. What these properties are trying to achieve is the action of a thick, stiff, heavy material.

5 Save your work

Making a garment

Once the panels are created, a garment can be made from them. Only one panel is turned into a garment and the remaining panels are seamed to the garment panel to create a single piece of clothing.

1 Make a panel into a garment

- Select a panel on the front of the robe.

- Select **Cloth → Create Garment**.

    The panel symbol should change into a garment symbol and a polygonal surface should be created. The surface will be bound by the panel curves.

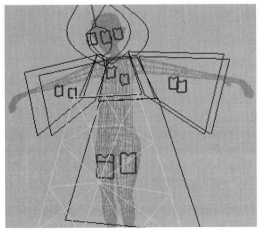

A garment created from a panel

2 Create a seam

Once a garment is created, edge curves should be selected to define a seam.

- Select a side curve of the front and rear bottom panels.

  Turning all objects off except for curves in the pick mask can make this task easier.

- Select **Cloth** → **Create Seam**.

  Icons should appear to represent the seam created and the polygonal surface should now wrap around to the back of the robe.

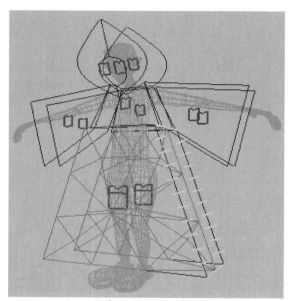

Seaming panels

3 Repeat step 2 until the entire garment is created

Do not seam together the opening in the front of the hood.

Switching to toggle shade mode can help you to see if you have missed any seams.

You may assign a different shader to the robe to get a better idea of the fit.

All seams have been created for the robe

4 Rename the garment

- Select the robe and rename it *robe*.

5 Transfer all the panels to a layer

6 Save your work

Relaxing the garment

The robe looks very primitive. The robe can be refined as you relax, or fit, the garment to Ichabod. To relax the garment you should specify a collision object, in this case Ichabod, and then run a number of simulations to achieve the proper fit.

1 Define Ichabod as a collision object

Ichabod should now have a shape node with two attributes; **Collision Offset** and **Collision Depth**. These two attributes should always be checked and changed, if necessary, before doing the initial simulation.

Tip: *Collision Offset* is how far away from the surface the cloth will try to be. *Collision Depth* is how far into the surface cloth can penetrate and be repelled. Both of theses attributes are measured in current maya units.

- Select *Ichabod*.
- Select **Cloth** → **Create Collision Object** and set the following:

    Set **Collision Offset** to **0.4**;

    Set **Collision Depth** to **1.0**.

    A robe should be a thick, bulky material. A value of 0.4 will keep it a good distance off the surface.

    With a character like Ichabod this may need some experimentation. Ichabod is one surface so you should look at the narrower parts of him to determine the depth. He is around 1.0 unit in the arms.

2 Adjust the resolution on the garment's panels

You'll notice areas where the robe penetrates the character. This is mainly due to the resolution of the panels (it can also be caused by poor panel alignment). The resolution should be increased on a panel by panel basis.

Smaller panels will usually need a higher resolution than larger panels, especially in the case of the main top panels that have panels connected to them on every side.

Panel resolution can usually be bumped up for oddly shaped panels as well. The hood panels are a good example of this.

- Select the two bottom panels.
- Change their **Resolution Factor** to **2** in the Channel Box.
- The other panels should have their resolutions changed as follows:

    Sleeves to **3**;

    Hood and upper panels to **4**.

    The robe should now look and fit better and without intersecting Ichabod.

Increased panel resolution

Tip: One thing that should always be checked is the *Solver Scale*. The cloth solver works in real world units. Since computer generated elements are not always built to scale this should be adjusted if necessary.

The default Maya units are centimeters and an average person is between 150 and 200cm in height. If you want to be specific, there are 2.54 centimeters in an inch.

Ichabod is about 21cm in height, so to convert him to the real world multiply his height by 10 to get 210cm. The solver scale should be set to 10.

Distance can be measured in Maya with **Create → Measure Tools → Distance Tool**.

---

3   Adjust the Solver Scale

Before running the simulation, the solver should have some attributes changed.

- Select the robe.

   This should list a solver in the **Inputs** section of the Channel Box.

- Name the solver *robeSolver*.

- Set the **Solver Scale** to **10**.

- Set **Gravity1** to **0**.

  When relaxing a garment it is a good idea to set **Gravity** to **0**. By default, Gravity1 is set to **-980**. This is to mimic real-world gravity.

- Set **Output Statistics** to **On**.

  If you want to track the amount of time a solution is taking you can turn **Output Statistics On**. It will tell you how long each frame takes to solve and how long the solver has been working in total.

4 Run a simulation

- Press the **Play** button.

  Let the simulation run for 20 or 30 frames. You can press **Stop** or the **Esc** key to end the simulation.

  You should see the robe shrink a bit to fit around Ichabod's body and take on more of a familiar shape.

A better fitting robe

If you look carefully, you should also see some bunching of the fabric on the front and back in the regions of the main panel. You should also see some problems with the hood. It may be bunching up or even sliding off of Ichabod's head.

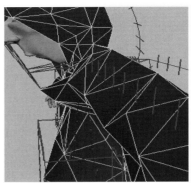

Bunching on the main panel

This happens based on the shape of the panels. This can be fixed interactively.

5 Add a stand-in object for Ichabod's head

Part of the problem with the hood fitting properly is the complexity of the head. The surface normals change direction many times and the ears and nose protrude a lot.

A stand-in object can be added to represent the head. It will give the hood a more uniform shape and the solver will work a little faster.

- Create a sphere with **12 sections** and **6 spans**.

- **Rename** the sphere *headStandIn*.

- Position and shape the sphere to Ichabod's head.

    This will require a combination of moving and scaling of the sphere and its CV's. The fit should be approximate and not labored over.

- Select **Cloth → Create Collision Object**, and set the following:

    Collision Offset to **0.4**;

    Depth to **1.0**.

    These are the same values as set on Ichabod. Generally, the offset values should be the same for each garment. Depth can vary based on the size of the collision object.

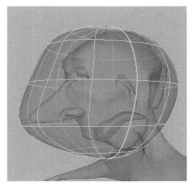

A stand-in object for the head

When animating Ichabod, the sphere should be parented into the neck skeleton hierarchy.

6 Run another simulation

- Rewind the Time Slider.

- Select **Simulation** → **Delete Cache**.

Note: When using the Time Slider to run a simulation, a cache file is created. If you want to resimulate, the cache should be deleted.

- Press the **Play** button.

  Stop the simulation when the robe has assumed a nice shape.

7 Save your work

Tweaking the fit of the garment

After initially relaxing a garment on a character, you can get a good idea of the fit. You may find some problems with the fit. Common problems are:

- Bunching up of the fabric;

- Fabric stretching too much or not enough fabric to fit around the character; and

- Elements such as sleeves and pant legs are too short or too long for the character.

The following method will show you how to do this by smoothing out the chest area of the robe.

1   **Rewind the simulation**

This will let you work on the robe in the default shape. If a panel curve changes shape, the simulation will need to be rerun so this also makes sure that you are at the start to do the next simulation.

2   **Modify the shape of the curves**

Typically, panels are rounded at seams where there are openings. The fabric must fit around a rounded shape, so what may look like a straight line on a curved surface will be a curved line when the surface is flattened out.

Adjusting your pick mask so that only curves are selected will help.

- **Scale** in the second and third CV's of the side curves of the main panels in the X direction.

   As you modify the curves you should see the garment recalculate its shape based on the change to the panel definition.

- **Scale** out the second and third CV's of the inside curves of the sleeves.

   By scaling the CV's the curves will continue to define a panel that is coplanar.

   Notice the shape between the panels that the curves now define. It should look like an ellipse with the ends pinched together.

Modified curves for arm seams

3   **Run another simulation**

Twenty frames should be enough to let you see if your tweaking was effective or not. You should be seeing a better fit.

Note: Unlike before, the cache file does not need to be deleted. If the garment shape is modified the cache will automatically be deleted.

---

4 Modify the hood curves

Rounding the curves of branching panels or making a pinched ellipse shape can also be applied to the hood connection curves.

The curves are straight lines that lie in an orthographic plane. This means that the **Scale Tool** will not work to shape them. In this case, you can use the **Move Tool**. Make sure that you use it in local mode. If you do not, the panel will disappear and you will get an error message like this:

```
// Warning: Invalid cloth panel(s): check for open or
non-planar panels. //
```

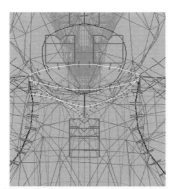

Modified curves for hood seams

5 Run another simulation

Remember to rewind to the start.

6 Increase the sleeve length

The sleeves should now be shorter than before. This is due to the change of the panel and how the seams bind the panels together better. The sleeve curves need to be moved out.

- Select the far edge curve of the sleeve and the two curves that share its corners.

- Select the edit points and **scale** them out in **X**.

  You could use the **Move Tool** but this is difficult to maintain symmetry with.

7 Increase the length of the bottom of the robe

- Select the edit points that define the bottom two panels of the robe.

- **Move** them down in **Y** to increase the overall length of the robe.

8 Run another simulation

After this simulation you should have the robe fitting quite well. You may notice a few things that do not look quite right. You can continue tweaking the garment until you are happy with the shape by following the above steps.

A better fitting robe

9 Increase the resolution

The next thing to do is to increase the resolution of the mesh. This will smooth out the robe and prepare it for use with animation.

- Scrub through the timeline until you find a frame that you like the fit of the robe.

  When choosing a frame, make sure that no vertices are inside of the geometry. You may see part of the geometry poke through the facets of the robe. This is acceptable and should be rectified by increasing the resolution.

- Select the robe.

- Select **Simulation** → **Save as Initial Cloth State**.

This will hold the current shape of the robe.

- Rewind the simulation.

The robe should not change shape.

- Open the Attribute Editor.

  Turn **Fit to Surface** to **On** for the *cpStitcher* node.

  Change the **Base Resolution** to **50**.

Tip: *Fit to Surface* applies to the resolution of the garment. If this option is turned on, the resolution of the garment will be increased and the current shape will be maintained as much as possible.

The robe should now have a much higher density. Notice the difference in resolution on the different panel areas. The bottom of the robe has a panel resolution of 2 whereas the top of the robe has a panel density of 4. Panels with many seams and panels that sit over geometry that will move a lot should have a higher resolution.

10 Add Gravity to the solver

Gravity will help to make the clothing sit more naturally.

- Select the *robeSolver*.

It should be accessible in the Channel Box as an input for the robe or in the Attribute Editor.

  Relax Frame Length to **5**;

  Gravity1 to **-980**.

Tip: *Relax Frame Length* ignores gravity for the specified number of frames. If a character has moved since the garment was last relaxed, you can use this to have some initial settling before gravity starts working.

This will pull the garment down in Y like real world gravity.

  Gravity2 to **-400**.

This will pull the garment slightly to the back so that it looks as if Ichabod is gliding forwards.

11 Run a simulation

Stop the simulation when you are satisfied with the look of the robe.

The final robe

12 Save your work

Summary

You have now created and relaxed a garment for a character. The basic workflow was:

- Create curves that define a closed shape;

- The curves are then converted into a panel and assigned properties;

- One panel is made into a garment;

- All other panels are seamed to the garment making one larger, complete garment;

- The character is defined as a collision object for the garment and solver attributes are set;

- The garment is relaxed to fit the character;

- Curves are tweaked to obtain a better fit.

A BATHROOM SCENE

This lesson will look at a bathroom scene and how cloth can be used to make various objects. You will learn how to use Transform Constraints to hang and place the shower curtain.

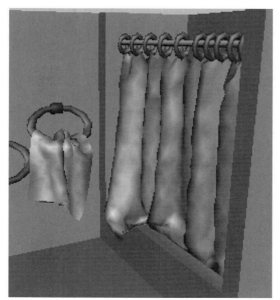

A bathroom scene

This lesson will focus on:

- Transform Constraints;
- Point assigners;
- Curve assigners;
- Drag manipulator.

Curtains and towels

Maya Cloth can be used to simulate things other than clothing. This lesson will look at creating a shower curtain and a towel for a bathroom scene.

Hang the shower curtain

A prominent element of a bathroom is the shower curtain. You will use Transform Constraints to hang the curtain from the curtain rod.

1 **Open a file**

- Open the file called *02.bathRoom*.

   This file has the bathroom created and a NURBS square for the curtain panel.

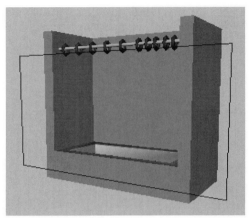

A bathroom scene

2 **Create a garment for the curtain**

- Select the four curves.

- Select **Cloth** → **Create Garment**.

- Rename *cpSolver* to *cpSolverCurtain*.

- Rename *cpStitcher* to *cpStitcherCurtain*.

- Rename *cpDefaultProperty* to *cpPropertyCurtain*.

- Increase the **Resolution** of the *cpStitcherCurtain* to **100**.

3 **Create locators**

- **Create** a locator.

- Snap the locator to the vertex starting one in from the end.

   You may want to template the tub and rod layers so that it is easier to see the locators and cloth vertices.

- Repeat this until you have one locator placed at every fourth vertex as shown.

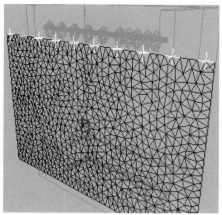

Locators snapped to vertices

4 Add Transform Constraints

Tip: A transform constraint can be added to a specific cloth vertex to hold it in space or to move it through space. Adding a transform constraint to a vertex (or vertices) creates a point assigner.

A point assigner will control points of a mesh that are constrained. The point assigner can be adjusted to constrain vertices within a specified radius.

Add Transform Constraints to vertices of the curtain by selecting a vertex and **Shift-selecting** a nearby locator.

- Select a vertex.
- **Shift-select** a locator.

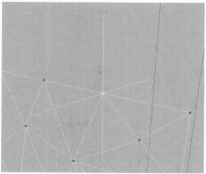

Selecting the vertex and locator

- Select **Constraints** → **Transform**.

A square icon should be added around the selected vertex to show that it is constrained.

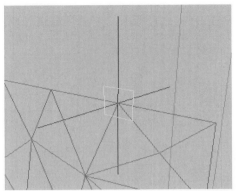

A constrained cloth vertex

- Repeat this until each locator is constraining a vertex.

5 Keyframe the locators

Now that the locators are constraining the curtain vertices, they can be keyframed over time so that they cause the curtain to hang from the rings on the curtain rod.

- Select all the locators.
- Set a key at frame **1**.
- Use the **MMB** in the Time Slider to set the current time to frame **30**.

  Using the **MMB** will not make the cloth solver update the curtain.

- **Move** the locators in **X** so that they line up with the curtain rings.
- Set a key at frame **30**.
- Set the current time to frame **60**.
- **Move** the locators in Y and Z so that they are positioned around the middle of the rings.
- Set a key at frame **60**.

  The keyframing of the locators is done with three keys instead of two. If the locators moved over only two frames, they would pass directly through the walls of the tub causing collision problems. Three keys gives you better control over the movement of the curtain.

6 Create a collision object

- Make the tub a collision object so that it interacts with the curtain.

Note: When setting up a collision object such as the tub, make sure that the surface normals are all pointing outwards.

---

7 Relax the curtain

- Adjust the following solver attributes:

    Relax Frame Length to **0**;

    Solver Scale to **10**.

    The relax frame length may be set to **0** as the curtain is in a relaxed shape already.

- Let a simulation run for at least **60** frames.

    This will ensure that the constrained vertices have been moved to the specified rings.

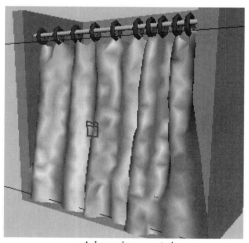

A hanging curtain

8 Save initial state for the curtain

- Move to a frame that you like the hang of the curtain.

- Select **Simulation** → **Save as Initial Cloth State**.

    The locators are still constraining the vertices and they should not be disabled unless the curtain should fall down. To make sure that they do not move you should delete the keyframes.

- Select the locators.
- **Edit → Delete by Type → Channels**.

  This will delete the animation from the locators and allow you to continue working from frame 1.

9 Parent the locators

If at any point you want the curtain to open, you should parent the locators to the rings. This will ensure that the curtain moves if the rings do.

10 Save your work

Drape the shower curtain

Now that the curtain is hanging from the shower rod, the bottom of the curtain can be placed in the tub. It can also be draped across the edge of the tub to add some visual stimulation to the scene.

1 Create a locator

- Create a locator with **Create → Locator**.
- Name it *curtainBottom*.
- Scale the locator to about the width of the curtain.

  This will help visualize what you can expect from keyframing the locator.

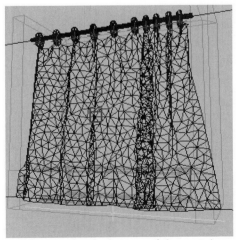

A locator for the bottom of the curtains

2 Add a transform constraint

This time you will make the transform constraint with a curve assigner. Curve assigners are created by constraining a panel curve.

Curve assigners will constrain every vertex on the edge of the panel even if the resolution of the panel or garment changes.

- Select the bottom curve of the curtain panel curves.
- **Shift-select** the *curtainBottom* locator.
- Select **Constraints → Transform**.

  You should see one square icon at each vertex along the bottom of the curtains.

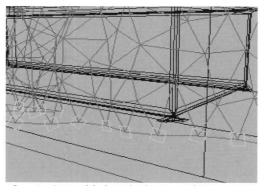

Constraints added to the bottom of the curtain

The curve assigner has a start and end parameter that can be used to constrain only part of an edge of a panel instead of the entire edge.

Since part of the curtain will stay outside of the tub, the curve assigner can be modified to affect only part of the curtain.

- Select the *curveAssigner1* in the Channel Box.
- Set the **End Param** to **0.8**.

3 Keyframe the locator

- Set a key for the *curtainBottom* locator at frame **1**.
- Move to frame **30** with the **MMB**.
- **Move** the *curtainBottom* locator above the edge of the tub and slightly into the tub.
- **Rotate** the locator in **Y** so that it straddles either end of the tub.
- **Scale** the locator in **X** so that it fits into the tub.

- Set a key at frame **30**.

  This will lift the bottom of the curtain up above the edge of the tub, squeeze it down so that it can fit into the tub and then turn it so that the side goes into the tub.

4 Run a simulation for 30 frames

You should see the curtain raised up as shown.

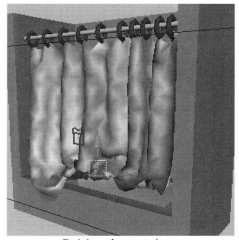

Raising the curtain up

5 Turn off the constraint

- Select one of the squares that represent the constraint.
- In the Channel Box, set **Constraint Weight** to **0**.

  This will stop the constraint from pulling on the curtain and allow it to fall down with the pull of gravity.

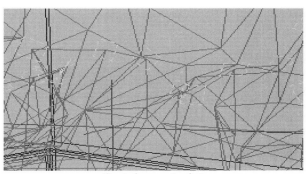

Curtain constraints

When the weight of the constraint is set to **0**, the outline of the boxes will be a dotted line.

6 Continue the simulation

Continue running the simulation for about **25** frames or until you are happy with the position of the curtains.

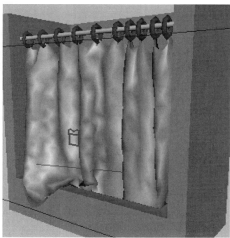

Lowering the curtain

7 Save your work

Hanging a towel

To complete the bathroom scene you will hang a towel from a ring. You will do this by using a new cloth solver and a variation of the transform constraint called a drag manipulator.

1 Disable the curtain solver

The simulation on the towel will run more quickly if the curtain solver is disabled.

- Select the curtain.

- Select **Simulation → Disable Solver**.

    Whatever frame you disable the solver at is the shape that it will hold throughout a playback so make sure that you like the look of the curtain when you disable the solver.

    The solver can also be disabled through the Attribute Editor.

    All scene elements but the towel, wall and towel ring can be hidden.

2 Create a new solver

You will use a second solver to create this towel. Each solver will have its own cache file. This allows you greater control over the scene by focusing on one piece of cloth at a time. This also helps to keep the scene well organized.

- Select **Simulation** → **Solvers** → **Create Solver**.

  This will become the active solver. The active solver will be marked in the solver menu.

3 Create a towel

- Display the *wall* layer.
- **Create** a new layer for the curtain curves and panel and hide it.
- **Create** a NURBS square that is about 8 x 14 units in size.
- Make the curves into a garment with **Cloth** → **Create Garment**.
- **Rename** *cpStitcher1* to *cpStitcherTowel*.
- Set the *cpStitcherTowel* **Resolution** to **100**.

  A new solver should be created for the towel so that its simulation will run more quickly and so that the curtain will not be disturbed.

Note: Garments can be moved into other solvers if desired with **Simulation** → **Transfer Garment**. In this case the new solver will be used to work with so that Maya runs more efficiently.

- **Rename** *cpSolver1* to *cpSolverTowel*.

  At this stage, it is also a good idea to assign the towel a new property.

- With the towel selected, **Simulation** → **Properties** → **Create Property**.
- **Rename** *cpProperty* to *cpPropertyTowel*.

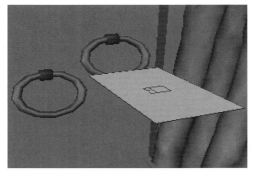
The towel created

4 Add a drag control manipulator

A drag manipulator is basically a transform constraint on a path. It can be used to pull on parts of a piece of cloth to shape or place it. You will use a drag manipulator to pull the towel through the towel ring.

- Select three edge vertices on the towel.

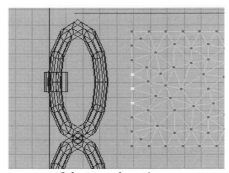
Select towel vertices

- Select **Simulation** → **Manipulators** → **Drag Control**.

  You will see a curve with a locator at one end and a shuttle at the other end. The locator controls the end of the curve and the shuttle controls the placement of the constraints when running a playback simulation. The *U Value* can be keyframed to move the shuttle along the curve.

  When running a local simulation, the movement along the curve is controlled by the shuttle's **Rate** attribute instead of the U *Value*.

- **Move** the locator and then the CV's of the curve to change the shape of the curve to look as shown.

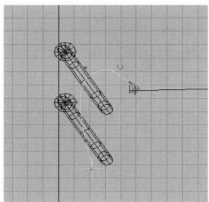

Drag manipulator

- Select the constraint icon and set the following options:

    Is Soft to **On**;

    Stiffness to **1000**.

Tip: *Is Soft* changes how the constraint pulls the cloth. With *Is Soft* turned Off the vertices will move with the constraint and maintain their positional relationship that existed at the time of creation.

With *Is Soft* turned On, the positional relationship can change, *Stiffness* will affect how much the relationship can change. The higher the value, the less the change.

The curtain had *Is Soft* turned Off so the unconstrained vertices off the cloth would move to meet the requirements of the panel properties. The towel has *Is Soft* turned On so that the towel is not stretched out of shape and maintains a more natural shape and movement.

---

5 Run a local simulation

Local simulation can be run to update only a certain garment. It is useful to run a local simulation when shaping an object prior to the final simulation when you will want to save the cache file.

- Select *cpSolverTowel* and set the following:

    Gravity1 to **0**;

    Solver Scale to **10**.

Note: When you create a new solver it will have default settings and the scale should be changed to match the other solvers in the scene.

- Make the wall, rings and floor collision objects.

  If an object has been declared a collision object for a solver and it is to be used in another solver you should make it a collision object for the new solver as well. A collision object only collides with objects that are in the solver that the collision object is defined in.

- Select **Simulation → Start Local Simulation**.

  Let the simulation run until the towel is about half way through the ring.

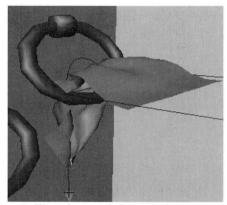

Pulling the towel through the ring

If the towel is not moving through the ring smoothly, you may have to adjust the shape of the drag manipulator curve so that is does move through smoothly.

6 Relax the towel into the ring

Now that the towel is through the ring it can have the resolution increased and be relaxed. The size of the towel can also be increased at this step.

- Select **Simulation → Save as Initial Cloth State**.
- Turn **Fit to Surface** to **On** for *cpStitcherTowel*.
- Set the **Resolution** on *cpStitcherTowel* to **200**.

Tip: Putting the towel through the ring is easier and quicker at a lower resolution.

- Set **Gravity1** to **-980** on *cpSolverTowel*.
- Set the following values on *cpPropertyTowel*:

    Thickness to **3**;

    Thickness Force to **20**.

    This will help to give the towel some thickness so that the wrinkles do not look like folded paper.

- Set a keyframe on **U** and **V scale** for the *cpPropertyTowel* at frame **1** at the default value of **1**.
- Set a keyframe on **U** and **V scale** for the *cpPropertyTowel* at frame **30** at a value of **1.5**.

    This will allow the size of the cloth to increase gradually over 30 frames. Because the towel is inside the ring, increasing the scale of the cloth immediately could cause penetration problems.

- Perform a playback simulation for at least 30 frames.

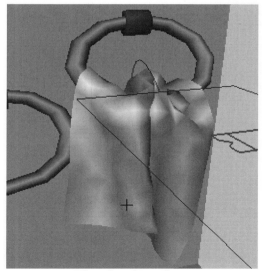

The relaxed towel

7 Save your work

Summary

You have now examined some concepts for shaping and manipulating cloth with Transform Constraints. You have also looked at the drag manipulator which is a variation of the transform constraint. As you continue, remember that point and curve assigners are used by the other constraint types that you will see in future lessons.

You have also used multiple solvers in a scene to control a complex scene with greater ease and organization.

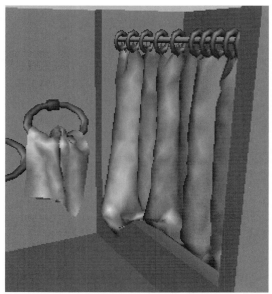

The completed scene

An object such as the curtain or towel may be static in the scene. In the lesson the solver was disabled so that it would not have to perform any unnecessary calculations.

If you are happy with the look of an object that will not move you can further simplify it by deleting history (**Edit → Delete by Type → History**).

MAKING OVERALLS

This lesson will show how to make overalls for Ichabod. Cloth and mesh constraints will be focused on as they are important to the success of the overalls. Button constraints will also be used to add some extra style to the overalls.

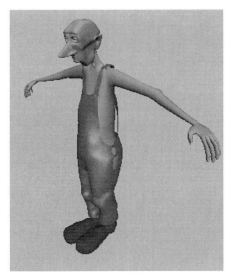

Create overalls

The workflow to create this robe will be covered, including:

- Adding cloth constraints;
- Adding mesh constraints;
- Adding button constraints.

Shoulder straps and buttons

In this lesson you will make overalls for Ichabod. Overalls have two important features:

- shoulder straps; and
- button closures at the sides.

These features can be simulated with Maya Cloth using *cloth, mesh,* and *button* constraints.

Create curves for the overalls

Curves need to be created to define the panels for the overalls. The overalls created here are a fairly simple design.

1 Open a file

- Open the file called *01.IchabodCharacter*.

2 Import the curves

Since you have gone through the procedure of creating curves for a garment in the first lesson, you can import most of the curves for the overalls.

- Import the file called *03.overallsCurves*.

  You will notice that the curves for the rear straps of the overalls are missing.

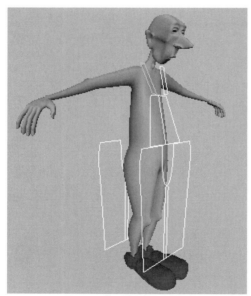

Curves for the overalls

3 Create back strap curves

The workflow to create a panel such as this is worth looking at. The main curves are created and then broken and filleted to make the final panel curves.

- Create curves as shown.

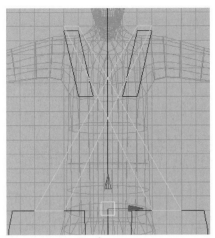

Back curves

The curves need to be open in the center so that they define one closed shape. To do this, you should break the curves and fillet them to ensure that they make a closed shape.

4 Break the curves

- Select the four, long curves that cross in the middle.

  The other curve groups can now be hidden.

- Press **F8** to go to component mode.

- Set the pick mask to select curve points.

- **Shift-select** four curve points as shown.

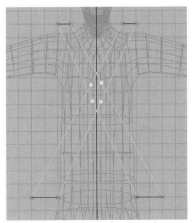

Curve points for detach

- Select **Edit Curves** → **Detach Curves**.

  The four curves should now be eight curves.

5 Fillet the curves

- Select two curve points as shown.

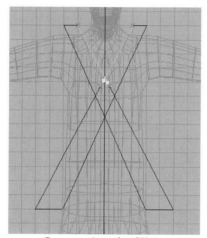

Curve points for fillet

- Select **Edit Curves** → **Curve Fillet - ❏**, and set the following options:

  Trim to **On**;

  Radius to **0**.

- Press **Fillet**.

  You should see that the two curves now come to a point.

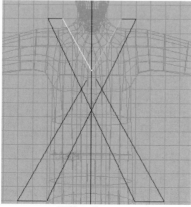

Filleted curves

| Note: | Fillet may not work exactly as shown here. If it does not, you should be able to use this technique to determine the four points of the diamond in the centre. You can then snap to curve points to create the closed shape. |

---

6 Continue filleting

Fillet all the curves until you have a closed shape for the back straps.

If you have trouble with a fillet, you may find it easier to mirror the curves to define the opposite side of the straps.

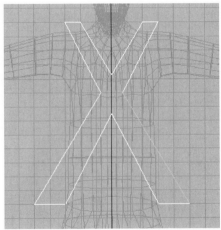

All fillets completed

7 Group and name the curves

- **Group** and name the curves *backCurves*.

    You may want to align these curves more closely to the character at this point.

Create panels and garments

Now that the curves are defined, the panels and garments can be created. Unlike the robe, the overalls will be made of two garments. The pants portion will be one garment and the straps will be the other.

1 Make a garment from a group of leg curves

Curves can be made into a garment directly. They do not need to be made into a panel first.

- Select one group of legs curves.
- Select **Cloth → Create Garment**.

  This should only be done to one of the curve groups. The others will be made into panels that will be seamed to this one.

- **Rename** *cloth1* to *clothPants*.
- **Rename** the *cpStitcher* to *cpStitcherPants*.

2 Make a garment from the back straps curves

The back strap curves will also be made into a garment. The overalls will be made of two garments that are cloth constrained together.

- Select the back straps curves.
- Select **Cloth → Create Garment**.

  If you get an error like the following, you may have empty curves in the *backCurves* group.

  ```
  // Error: Curves must be coplanar.  Check for out of
  plane control vertices. //
  ```

  Delete the curves and try to make the garment again.

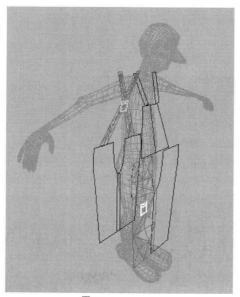

Two garments

- **Rename** *cloth2* to *clothStraps*.

- **Rename** the *cpStitcher1* to *cpStitcherStraps*.

3 Make the other panels

All remaining curve groups should be made into panels.

Adding all panels to a layer at this point is a good idea.

4 Assign a property to the panels

- Select all the panels.
- Select **Simulation** → **Properties** → **Create Cloth Property**.

5 Seam the panels together

- Seam the two front strap panels to the back straps garment.

  Do not seam the straps into the main garment. They will be attached with constraints later on.

- All the other panels can be seamed together.

  Do not seam together the top edges of the pants. This part of the overalls will also be closed with constraints.

- A new shader can be applied to the garments at this point.

6 Increase the density of the garments

The garments are not dense enough in some places. You can see the leg geometry poking through the pants and the definition of the straps is rough. By changing the resolution of the panels and or stitchers, this can be improved.

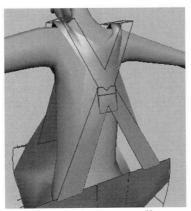

Low resolution overalls

- Change the **Resolution** on the pant leg panels to **4**.

  This should give the legs of the overalls a better shape.

- Change the **Resolution** of the *cpStitcherStraps* to **100**.
- Change the **Resolution** of the straps panels to **2**.

  The straps should now look more like the curves that define them.

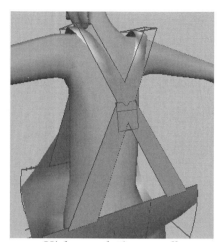

Higher resolution overalls

7 Save your work

Add mesh constraints to the straps

Mesh constraints connect parts of a garment to a polygon mesh. They can be used to attach cuffs to ankles and wrists. Mesh constraints can also be used to add accessories to characters like ties, hats and jewelry.

Mesh constraints will be used to attach the straps to Ichabod's shoulders so that they do not fall off when he moves.

The mesh constraints will also help to keep the straps from stretching too thinly or bunching up over the shoulders.

1 Move the straps

If you look at the straps from the front, you should see some penetration through the shoulders. Penetration will make a decent solution more difficult

- **Move** the straps forward approximately **0.5** in **X**, so that they fit comfortably over the shoulders.

Straps moved forward

2 Save as Initial Cloth State for the straps

Since the *clothStraps* have been moved, their initial state should be saved so that the constraint positions can be calculated accurately.

- Select **Simulation** → **Save as Initial Cloth State**.

3 Make Ichabod a collision object

Collision objects need to be defined before cloth can be constrained to them.

- Select *Ichabod*.
- Select **Cloth** → **Create Collision Object** and set the following:

    Collision Offset to **0.3**;

    Collision Depth to **1.0**.

4 Add a mesh constraint

To add a mesh constraint, you must select cloth vertices followed by the mesh object and then create the constraint.

- Select *clothStraps*.
- Use the **RMB** to switch to vertex select mode.
- In the side view, select the vertices as shown.

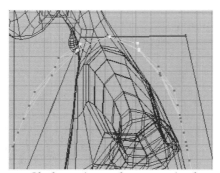

Cloth vertices to be constrained

- **Shift-select** *Ichabod*.

- Select **Constraints** → **Mesh**.

  You should see squares on the straps at the vertex positions.

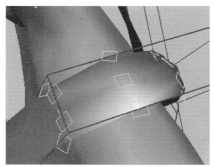

Mesh constraint added

  If you did not save the initial state for the straps before adding the constraint, you will see the icons behind the straps instead of on them.

- **Rename** the *meshConstraint1* to *shoulderConstraint*.

Add cloth constraints to connect the garments

As mentioned before, the garments will be connected together using cloth constraints.

Cloth constraints allow you to constrain vertices of a garment to the same garment or another garment. The straps will be constrained at both ends to the pants portion of the overalls. Using constraints to make the connection will work better than using seams. Seams work best when the edges being seamed are a similar length. The straps are much narrower than pants. If these panels were seamed together, the longer edges of the pants would bunch up like ruffles or pleats to fit the size of the seam.

Another benefit of using cloth constraints is that the state of the constraints can be animated. If you needed to undo one of the straps, constraints would make this possible.

1 Move the clothStraps vertices closer to the clothPants

Cloth constraints will constrain the vertices to the closest piece of the constraint cloth. To ensure a precise connection placement of the straps they can be moved before adding the constraint.

- Select vertices on the front of the straps as shown.

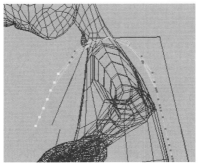

Move these vertices

- Select **Modify** → **Transformation Tools** → **Proportional Modification Tool** - □.
- Set the following options:

    Modification Falloff to **Linear**;

    Distance Cutoff to ~**1.3** (based on distance in Y).

- Set the pivot point of the vertices to the bottom vertices.
- Move the vertices so that they line up with the top, front part of the overalls.

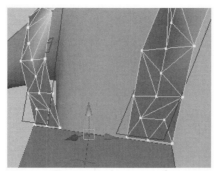
Front vertices moved

- Repeat this for the vertices on the back of the straps.

  They should line up as shown.

Rear vertices moved

2 Update the cloth state

When vertices of a cloth object are manually moved, the state of the cloth should be updated.

- Select **Simulation** → **Update Cloth State**.

3 Add cloth constraints

- Select a curve from the straps front panel.

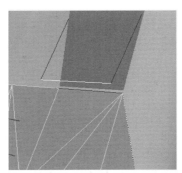

Select a panel curve

- **Shift-select** the *clothPants* mesh.

- Select **Constraints** → **Cloth**.

  You should see square icons added to the cloth like you did when adding the mesh constraint.

- Repeat this for the three other parts of the straps.

Relax the garment and add more constraints

The goal of this step is to add buttons to close the sides of the overalls. Before adding the constraints, the garment should be relaxed so that you have an idea of where to add the constraints.

1 Run a simulation

- Run a playback simulation to relax the overalls. Five to ten frames should be sufficient.

- Turn Output Statistics **On** to get information about the solve and Cloth Collisions **Off** to increase the speed.

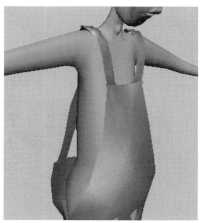

Relaxed overalls

2 Increase the resolution of the pants

You will likely see the legs sticking through the pants.

- Increase the **resolution** on the *cpStitcherPants* to **50**. Make sure that you turn Fit To Surface **On** before changing the resolution.

3 Modify the shape of the pants

- **Move** two vertices on either side of the *clothPants* to look as shown.

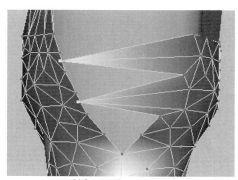

Side vertices moved

These vertices will be cloth constrained to close the sides of the overalls.

- Select **Simulation** → **Update Cloth State**.

Every time vertices are manually moved, the cloth state should be updated.

4 **Add cloth constraints**
  ▪ Select **Constraints** → **Cloth**.

5 **Relax the garment again**
  ▪ Be sure to delete the cache from the previous simulation and to save the initial state of the *clothStraps* and *clothPants* before running the simulation.

    Ten to fifteen frames should be enough to relax the garment.

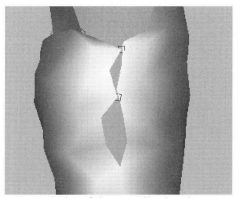

Sides of the overalls closed

  ▪ Save the initial state of the clothing at a frame you like.

Add button constraints

The overalls are basically finished. They can be improved cosmetically, though. The finishing touch for the overalls will be to add buttons for the straps and the side closures.

1 **Create a button**

  Buttons can be as simple or as complex as you desire. You will generally want to keep them simple as they are not usually a major focus in a scene.

  ▪ Select **Create** → **Polygons Primitives**→ **Cylinder**.
  ▪ **Rename** the cylinder to *button*.
  ▪ **Scale** the *button* to approximately **0.13, 0.03,** and **0.13**.
  ▪ Change the **Subdivisions X** to **12**.

    You may want to add a shader to the button at this point.

2 **Duplicate and place the buttons**

  ▪ Make five duplicates of the button.

You will use two for the straps and two for each side of the overalls. Placement will be a combination of rotation and translation.

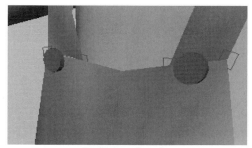

Buttons placed

3 Add button constraints

Button constraints are almost the opposite of mesh constraints. Instead of constraining the cloth to an object, an object is constrained to the cloth.

- Select all the *buttons*.
- **Shift-select** the *clothPants*.
- Select **Constraints** → **Button** - ❒. Set the following options:

    Preserve Translation to **Off**;

    Preserve Rotation to **On**.

- Press **Create**.

    The buttons should move to the surface of the overalls and maintain their rotation.

4 Increase the resolution of the pants and simulate again

- Increase the **resolution** of the *cpStitcherPants* to **100**.
- Increase the **resolution** of the top front panels to **2**.

    After ten or fifteen frames the overalls should be relaxed into a nice shape.

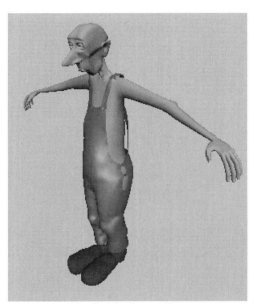

The finished overalls

5 Save your work

Summary

You have now created overalls for a character and utilized cloth, mesh and button constraints to complete the garment.

Cloth and mesh constraints are important for putting garments together and fitting them to a character. Button constraints are best for aesthetic finishing.

If you would like to review working with constraints further, try to add a pocket to the front or back of the overalls.

BLOWING A HAT AWAY

This lesson will show how to make a hat for Ichabod. Once the hat is created, fields will be used to blow it off of Ichabod's head.

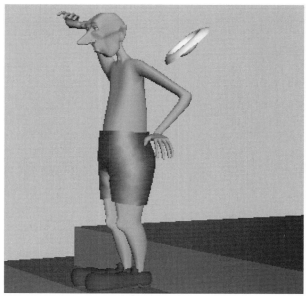

A blowing hat

The following topics will be covered, including:

- Creating cloth objects;

- Adding field constraints.

Making a hat blow away

You will make a hat for Ichabod from NURBS geometry and then have it blow away using some dynamic fields in this lesson.

Make a hat

For this tutorial a hat will be built from NURBS geometry and converted into a cloth object.

1 Open a file

- Open the file called *04.hatScene*.

2 Create a hat

- Create a curve above Ichabod's head like the one shown below.

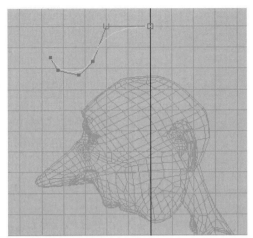

Curve for hat

- **Revolve** the hat about the **Y-axis**.
- Convert the hat to a polygon surface with **Modify** → **Convert** → **NURBS to Polygons** - ☐.
- Set the following options:

  U Type to **Per Span # of Iso Params**;

  Number U to **4**;

  V Type to **Per Span # of Iso Params**;

  Number V to **4**.
- Press **Tessellate**.

  At this stage you may want to adjust the construction history of the polygon object so that it has an even distribution of faces. Unlike the cloth garments, the resolution of cloth objects cannot change.
- **Hide** the NURBS curve and surface.
- **Delete History** on the polygon hat.
- **Rename** the polygon hat to *hat*.

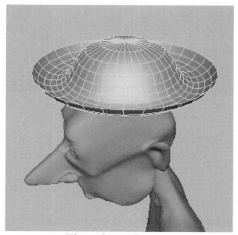

The polygon hat

3 Move the hat onto the head

- **Move** the hat down in **Y** so that it is closer to Ichabod's head.

  You may want to use **Modify → Center Pivot** to center the manipulator on the hat.

4 Scale the hat to better fit the head

- **Scale** the hat in the **X-axis** so that it better conforms to the shape of Ichabod's head.

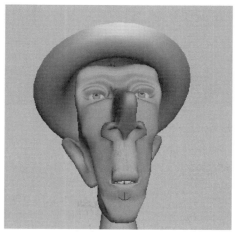

Scale the hat in X

5 Merge edges on the hat

If you look closely at the front brim of the hat, as pictured below, you will see a hard edge. The edges of these polygons are not connected and produce a hard edge. If this is not fixed before the simulation is run there will be a tear in the front of the hat.

Unconnected polygon edges

- Select **Edit Polygons** → **Merge Edge Tool**.
- Click on an edge of the hat.

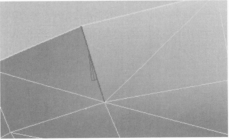

Select an edge

- Click on the edge again and press **Enter** to validate the command.

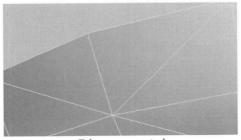

Edges connected

6 Create a cloth object

- With the hat selected, select **Cloth** → **Create Cloth Object**.

This will convert the hat to a cloth object and connect it to a cloth solver and property.

7 Save your work

Add constraints to the hat

Constraints can now be added to the hat and a simulation can be run to test out the setup.

Field constraints work a little bit differently than in the traditional dynamics solver. Like the other cloth constraints, vertices are selected and then connected to the desired field.

1 Adjust the solver

The solver scale and frame rate should be adjusted. You will remember from the previous lessons that a solver scale of 10 was used with Ichabod.

The hat was created in its desired shape so unlike a garment it does not need an initial relax frame length so it can be set to **0**.

Cloth collisions can be turned **Off** for the hat as it will likely not be colliding with itself or other cloth objects.

2 Adjust the hat properties

The hat can be made into a fairly stiff object by using the following settings:

Bend Resistance to **100**;

Stretch Resistance to **100**;

Shear Resistance to **100**;

Bend Rate to **1**.

3 Make Ichabod a collision object

4 Add a field constraint to the hat brim

- Create an air field with **Fields → Air**.

  Make sure that no objects are selected when you create the air field so that they are not converted to a rigid body and connected to the field.

- Move the field up around Ichabod's head.

- Set the following options on the air field so that it will blow the hat backwards and up off of Ichabod's head:

  Magnitude to **500**;

  Attenuation to **0**;

  Direction X to **0**;

  Direction Y to **0.3**;

  Direction Z to **-1**.

- Select some vertices on the brim of the hat as shown.

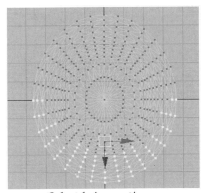

Select brim vertices

- **Shift-select** the air field.
- Select **Constraints** → **Field**.

  Constraint icons will be added to the hat.

5 **Run a simulation**

6 **Save your work**

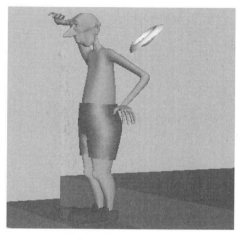

The hat blowing away

Summary

You have now created a cloth object from NURBS geometry and connected it to a dynamic field.

If you want to review working with dynamic fields further, try to add some turbulence to the hat or make the shorts blow in the wind.

TEXTURING CLOTH

This lesson will show various texturing techniques, including:

- Projection mapping;
- The Texture View window;
- Creating a double sided shader.

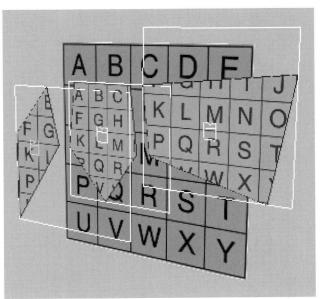

Cloth texture mapping is based on a bounding box

Texturing

Texturing cloth requires knowledge of texturing polygons and how cloth garments are initially texture mapped. The two main concepts to know are:

- Polygon Projection Mapping;
- The UV Texture Editor.

This lesson will look at these issues and how to work with them.

Texture placement

Cloth panels are textured by the size of the panel's bounding box. In the image below, a square texture is applied to a square plane and three non-square panels. Each panel has a square bounding box that the texture fits into. The texture is placed from the lower left corner of the panel.

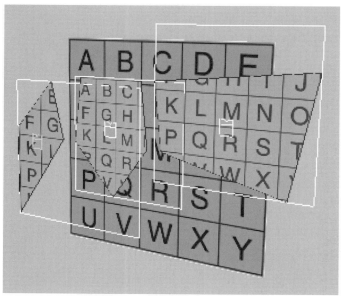

Texture based on bounding box

This is illustrated in the file *05.textureGrid*.

When the panels are seamed together they will appear as shown below. There will be noticeable breaks in the texture at the edges of the panels. This is due to the initial position of the panels.

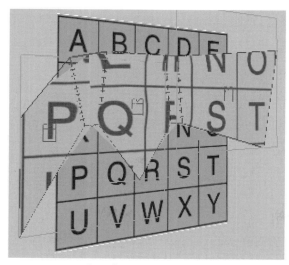

Panels seamed together

This can be fixed in the UV Texture Editor (Window Æ UV Texture Editor...) This will show you how the cloth mesh is being mapped and will let you fix the texture mapping.

Edit textures in the UV Texture Editor

The mapping of the cloth mesh in the pictures above can be edited so that there are no noticeable seams. Following is a sample workflow with the UV Texture Editor.

1 Open a file

- Open the file called *05.textureGrid*.
- Press **6** to go into texture mode.

2 Seam the panels together

- Seam the three blue colored panels together.

  You may hide the green plane and bounding box curves through the Layer Editor.

3 Set-up the UV Texture Editor

- Open **Window → UV Texture Editor...**

  You should see the UV Texture Editor window open with nothing in it but a grid.

- Select the seamed together object.
- Make sure **Image → Display Image** is checked **On**.
- Select *cloth1* to edit its texture coordinates.

  The UV Texture Editor window should look as shown below.

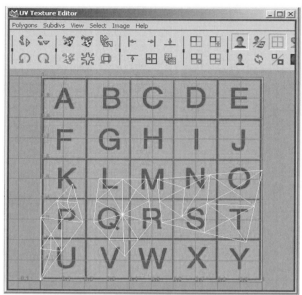

The UV Texture Editor window

Notice the separation between the panels even though they have been sewn into one garment. This window is displaying the texture coordinates which did not change when the seams were added.

4 Move texture vertices

- Press **F8** to switch to component mode.

- Turn all components **Off** except for *Poly UVs*.

  This will allow you to pick poly texture vertices so that you can fit the texture to the panels.

- Select and **Move** the top left vertex of the right panel.

  The vertex should be moved to the left so that it is in between its original position and the position of the top right vertex of the middle panel.

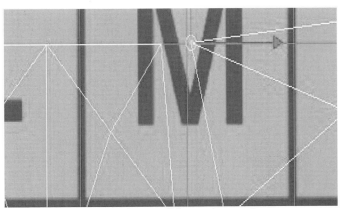

Move Tool to modify texture vertices

- Repeat the above steps until the texture coordinates line up without a seam or gap. Point snap can be used to line up the texture vertices.

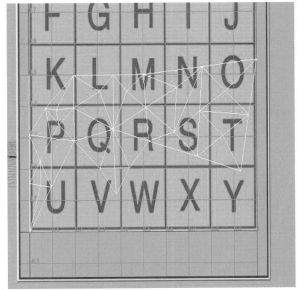

All vertices moved

When this is completed the texture should look better on the garment.

It is important to note that this should be one of the final steps in creating clothing. If you change the resolution of the garment you risk losing some of the modifications you have made to the texture coordinates.

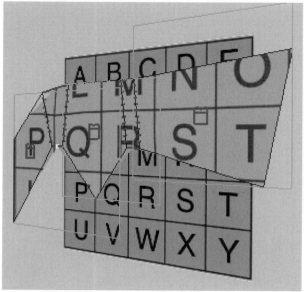

Texture coordinates moved

5 Save your work

Polygon Projection Mapping

As seen above, polygons have texture coordinates applied to them at the time of creation. The Texture View window is one way to change the texture coordinates.

Another way to modify texture coordinates is with projection mapping. Projection mapping applies texture coordinates to selected facets based on a planar, cylindrical or spherical projection.

The following steps go through the procedure of adjusting the texture coordinates on a sleeve.

1 Open a file

This arm is set on an angle and the garment was built around the sleeve on an angle.

- Open the file called *05.armProjection*.

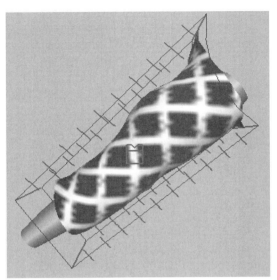

Texture on a sleeve

Notice that the grid texture on the arm is on the same angle that the panel curves were created at. The texture is mapped through the bounding box which is not on an angle.

2 Apply a projection map

- Select the facets of the shirt.
- Select **Edit Polygons → Texture → Cylindrical Mapping.**

This will create a manipulator around the sleeve.

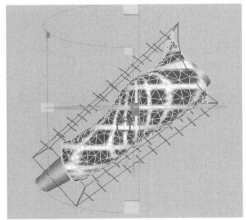

Cylindrical mapping manipulator

3 Adjust the manipulator

The manipulator can be moved, rotated and scaled to better fit the sleeve. The manipulator has a switch on one corner that will let you switch between texture placement and texture mapping. Click on it to change modes.

- Fit it around the sleeve so that the grid texture runs parallel to the panel curves.

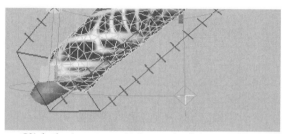

Click the icon to switch manipulator modes

The sleeve should look as pictured below after modifying the manipulator.

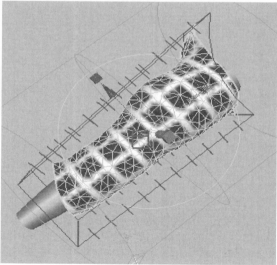

Texture coordinates fixed

4 Save your work

Double-sided textures

To create a garment with real thickness requires an inside and an outside surface. This can add extra time to building and solving the garment. One way to get around this is to create a double-sided texture as outlined in the following workflow.

1 Create two texture nodes

- Open the Hypershade **Window → Rendering Editors → Hypershade...**

- Create a *Checker* texture by selecting **Create → 2D Textures → Checker** and then **MMB** clicking in the Work Area of the Hypershade.

- Create a *Cloth* texture using the same method.

2 Create a Material

- Create a Blinn material node.

3 Create two utility nodes

- Select **Create → General Utilities → Condition** to create a *Condition* utility node.

- Create a *Sampler Info* utility node using the same method.

4 Make some connections

- **MMB** drag the *SamplerInfo1* node onto the *Condition1* node.

  This will open the Connection Editor with the *samplerinfo1* node loaded in the Output column, and the *condition1* node loaded in the input column. Connections can then be made by highlighting an attribute in the Output column and then an attribute in the Input column.

  The Connection Editor can also by opened by **Window → General Editors → Connection Editor...**

- **Connect** the **flippedNormal** attribute from the *samplerInfo1* to the **secondTerm** attribute of the *condition1* node.

- Select the *Checker1* texture and press the **Reload Left** button to load it into the Outputs column.

- **Connect** the *outColor* from the *checker1* texture to the **color1** attribute of *condition1*.

- Select the *Cloth1* texture and press the **Reload Left** button to load it into the Outputs column.

- **Connect** the *outColor* from the *cloth1* texture to the *color2* of *condition1*.

- Press the **Clear All** button to clear the Connection Editor.

- Load the *Condition1* utility node as the output, and the *blinn1* material node as the input.

- **Connect** the *outColor* from the *condition1* node to the *color* of the *blinn1* node.

- Select **Graph → Rearrange Graph** to clean up the Hypershade.

5 Test the shader

- Assign the shader to a 180 degree cylinder.

- Add an **Ambient Light** to the scene to illuminate the cylinder.

- Tumble the camera so that both sides of the cylinder can be seen and render to see a different texture on either side.

   The results of this can only be seen in a software render.

Summary

In this lesson you have looked at a couple of ways of modifying texture coordinates on a garment. You have also looked at an effective way of creating a double sided shader.

A COLLARED SHIRT

This lesson will look at creating a complex shirt with collar, pocket and buttons. It is more of a case study than a step by step guide to building a shirt. The focus is on portions of the shirt as they contribute to the whole shirt.

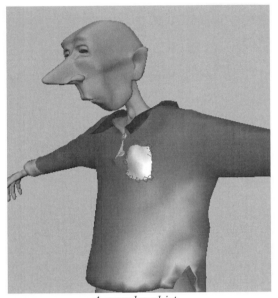

A complex shirt

Areas of focus include:

- Working with patterns;
- Creating thickness;
- Useful cloth properties.

Complex garments

Complex garments are relative to one's experience with cloth but there are elements of the design that can make a piece of clothing more complex. Things like buttons, pockets, cuffs and collars can all add up to a garment that is more challenging to create.

The file that explores the following concepts is called *06.IchabodCollar*.

Working from a pattern

Working from an established fashion pattern can be an appealing thing for a person lacking in fashion design experience. A pattern will give you a good idea of what the garment will look like before you start making it and help you to stay on track with that look.

Working from a pattern can simplify things and make them more difficult at the same time. A pattern will give you a good idea of how the different pieces of the cloth should be cut but it can also create more or less pieces than you may need.

The pattern for parts of this shirt might look like:

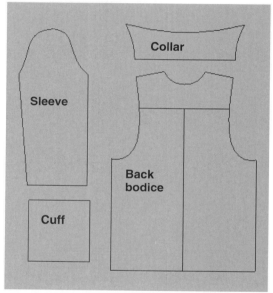

A typical shirt pattern

There are two main differences between traditional garment making and making clothes with Maya Cloth:

- folding; and
- texturing.

In traditional garment making pieces of cloth are often folded over themselves. This allows for fewer pieces of fabric to be cut.

Fabric also has coloring and texturing that must be considered when cutting a pattern. If a striped shirt were being made the stripes on the sleeve should generally go in the same direction as the stripes on the bodice (the bodice is the part of the shirt that goes around the torso).

Fabric also has a grainline which can determine the direction in which it is cut.

With computer generated cloth these considerations are quite the opposite. Texturing can be easily changed and folding can be difficult to achieve.

With this in mind, the pattern for this shirt could be modified to something like:

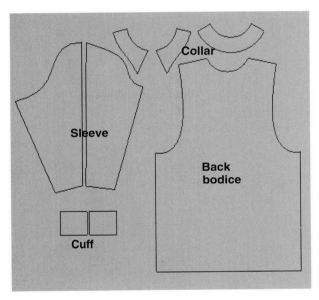

A shirt pattern modified for Maya Cloth

The bodice for the back of the shirt can be one piece instead of three. If the T-shape of the seams from the real-world shirt are desired, they can be created with the appropriate texture maps.

The sleeve must be cut into two pieces as a panel cannot be seamed to itself. The cuff is cut in half like the sleeve.

The collar must also be made in more pieces. This shirt has three pieces for the collar. In real life, one piece of material can be sewn to many but this is not so with Maya Cloth.

Even if one piece could be sewn to many it would likely not be beneficial in this case. Since cloth must fit around the character a more accurate fit can be created by using multiple pieces that can be placed around the character.

Creating thickness

Creating thickness on single surfaces is a problem common to all forms of computer graphics. With cloth, garments can very often look as if they are made of paper. If you are lucky, you can avoid close-ups or camera angles that will make this more visible. You may also be able to disguise this lack of thickness with shader and/or light assignment. Another possibility is blur in the form of depth of field or motion blur if you have the rendering resources available.

If none of these techniques will work for you, you will have to double up surfaces to create thickness. This creates more work for the solver and slows down the simulation so it should only be done when absolutely necessary.

The pattern for this shirt can be modified once more to use the technique of doubling surfaces to create thickness:

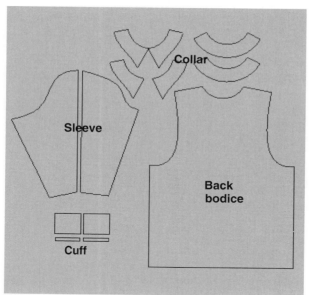

The pattern modified for thickness

This shirt has three pieces for the collar that are duplicated to create thickness and a smaller strip is created to represent the inside of the cuff.

Thick collar

One thing to be careful of when doing this is to make sure that the surfaces are not interpenetrating each other. If penetration occurs, the easiest way to hide it is to apply a transparent shader to the affected polygon faces.

Penetration can also be avoided in places like cuffs by making the inside surface slightly smaller in size. If you look at the panels of this shirt you should see that was done here.

Note: Adding shaders to facets should be the final step in the garment creation workflow.

Alternatives to the transparent shader include: adjusting panel properties, increasing solver frame samples and repositioning vertices and saving their new initial state.

Note: Avoiding creating thickness at the cuffs and collars will definitely keep garments on a simpler level. You can also select your cloth object and do a poly extrude to add thickness to the overall appearance.

Thickness property

The thickness property is not specific to creating thickness as mentioned above but it certainly helps. The thickness property pushes pieces of cloth apart from each other.

With this shirt the thickness helps to keep the two pieces of the collar separated except at the edges where they are sewn together. It is also useful to keep in mind when trying to get wrinkles in fabric.

There are two important things to know about thickness. The first is that the thickness attribute is divided by the solver scale. If you have increased the solver scale you may need to increase the thickness.

The second thing to know is that thickness is not additive. If two pieces of cloth collide, the higher thickness value will be used.

In this scene, the shirt has a thickness of **0.5** and a thickness force of **30**.

Measuring tools

The use of the Distance Tool (**Create** → **Measure Tools** → **Distance Tool**) to measure the height of a character and determine the scale of the solver has been discussed previously. In some situations, it may be used to measure the length of an arm or a panel so that the cloth fits properly.

Measuring a curve at a shoulder can be done with the Arc Length Tool (**Create** → **Measure Tools**→ **Arc Length Tool**). The curves that define connections in these regions are usually rounded.

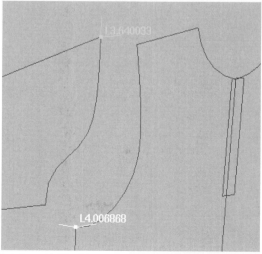

Arc Length Tool to measure shoulder panel curves

By applying an Arc Length locator at the end of each curve, feedback on the length of the curve is provided and the curves can be made to be the same length. It is important for curves to have similar lengths so that the cloth does not bunch up or pull the garment into a strange fit.

Curve degree

The degree of a curve determines how many CV's it will have. A degree 1 curve will have two CV's whereas the default degree 3 curve has four CV's. Degree 1 curves can be used where the panel edge is a straight line.

The benefit of using a degree 1 curve is apparent when tailoring the garment (or adjusting curves). There are fewer points to deal with so editing is easier. The curve will also stay as a straight line if it is degree 1.

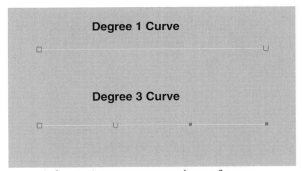

A degree 1 curve versus a degree 3 curve

If you think that the curve may have to be rounded use a degree 3 curve.

Crease angle

Crease angle is something that is very useful when creating collars and thickness for parts of a garment. Crease angle will put a noticeable edge where two panels meet. It is used on a collar to turn it down so that it is inclined to rest on the shoulders of the shirt or jacket it belongs to.

It also helps where two surfaces are being used to create thickness. Using an angle that will have some bend to the seam will give your cloth body.

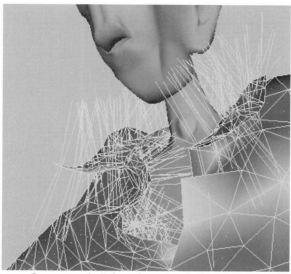

Crease angle is based on the cloth normals

Normals of a cloth mesh face the collision object at creation time. You can see above that the normals on the collar are facing opposite directions on the top and bottom of the collar. The crease angle in this case is 170.

The normals at the cuff are in the opposite alignment and have a crease angle of -150.

Positive crease angles turn the normals away from each other while negative values turn them towards each other.

Note: To display polygon normals use **Display → Polygon Components → Normals**.

Panel resolution

Panel resolution can be set independently of the stitcher resolution. It is useful to do this in more complex areas like the collar and cuffs to better define the shape of the cloth and to increase the accuracy of the simulation.

If the cloth is penetrating the collision object increasing the resolution can often fix it. Remember that it is the vertices of the cloth that are colliding with the collision object. Larger triangles (on a lower resolution garment) have a greater risk of the edges penetrating the collision object.

Panel placement

The placement of panels is an important consideration. When building the collar, the panels were moved as close to the neck as possible. This will get the shirt closer to a relaxed state and cut down on the work of the solver.

When the hem at the bottom of the shirt was created, it intersected with the rest of the shirt. It was rotated in towards the body so that the intersection did not occur.

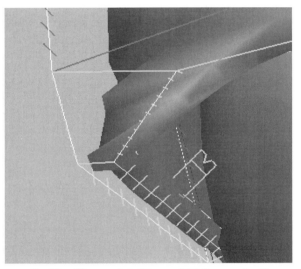

Inside of hem rotated to avoid interpenetration

The pocket was placed as close to the shirt as possible. If the pocket is too far from the surface it might not be constrained accurately. This means that it will not look like a well made pocket.

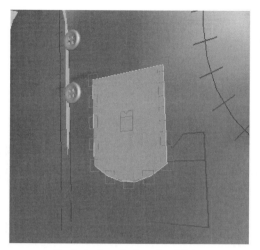

Pocket placed close to shirt

Multiple properties

This shirt uses multiple properties to control the behavior. The collar and button strip have much higher bend resistance settings to make them stiffer.

The collar also has a higher density to push it down onto the shirt.

Shiny shader

When this shirt was being built it had a shiny Blinn shader applied to it. This will help you evaluate the way in which the creases are forming and how material is wrinkling.

Work in steps

Working in steps or stages helps to speed up the workflow. When developing this shirt it was done in the following stages:

- create the bodice;
- create the collar;
- create a sleeve;
- create a cuff; and
- copy the existing sleeve and cuff for the other side of the shirt.

Working on parts of the garment helps you to stay organized and perhaps more importantly lessens the amount of work that the solver must do so that you get quicker feedback on if your design is going together as you desire.

The bodice is a good place to start as it is the main part of the garment and has all the other pieces attaching to it. If it fits properly, then tailoring the other components should be easy. If the whole garment is created as one piece it is much harder to isolate a problem in the shape or size of a panel.

The collar is generally the most complicated part of a garment and it is good to take care of it while the garment is relatively simple. The collar relies on the bodice for its placement so it is logical to work on as the second step.

Working on one sleeve and cuff at a time also keeps the amount of tweaking that you must do minimized. Take advantage of the symmetry that a sleeve offers and perfect one of them and then copy it for the opposite side.

Summary

Putting all these steps and workflows together makes creating a garment such as this easier. There are other ways in which things can be done and as you create your own garments you will discover them. Practice and experience will help you master Maya Cloth.

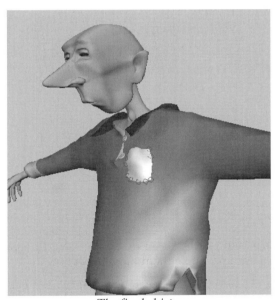

The final shirt

ANIMATED CHARACTERS

This lesson will show how to apply cloth to an animated character.

Ichabod animated with clothes

This lesson will focus on the following topics:

■ Exporting and importing garments;

■ The Bake Simulation tool;

■ Problem solving.

Adding cloth to an animation

Up until this point in the course, clothing has been created for Ichabod and he wears it like a mannequin. In this lesson, you will prepare some clothes for Ichabod to wear and make them move with him.

This is most easily accomplished by using multiple files and the following steps:

■ Animate a character;

■ Create clothes for the character;

■ Bake the animation onto the character's joints;

■ Refit the clothes; and

■ Simulate for the duration of the animation.

The order of the first couple steps may be switched and depending on how things work out, steps may be repeated.

Exporting garments

For the purpose of this lesson, pants and a shirt have been created for Ichabod.

1 Open a file

The shirt and pants in this scene are fairly simplistic and ready to be put onto the animated Ichabod. You may examine or change them at your leisure.

■ Select **File** → **Open**.

■ Open the file called *07.IchabodPantsShirt*.

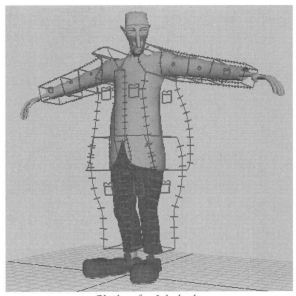

Clothes for Ichabod

There are two notable things with this file. The first is that when the pants were created, cloth collisions were turned off until the legs were relaxed enough to not interpenetrate each other.

The other important thing is that this file uses two cloth solvers; one for the pants and one for the shirt. There are two reasons for using multiple solvers. One reason is that you can work on one piece of clothing at a time. The other reason is to achieve the layering of the clothes. The shirt is over top of the pants. The pants used a collision offset of **0.15** while the shirt used an offset of **0.3** so that it would be outside of the pants.

2 Delete unnecessary nodes

- Select all the nodes that are not needed for the clothing. This includes:

  Ichabod;

  his skeleton, deformers and controls; and

  the lights and cameras.

  Do not delete the clothing, panels or panel curves. If you have to adjust the clothing you will need this data. The panels will be especially useful when you are adjusting the animation.

- **Delete** the selected nodes.

  An alternate way of doing this is to select the nodes you want to keep and use **File → Export Selection...**

3 Save as a new file

- Select **File → Save as**.

- Enter a name like *exportedClothing*.

  The clothes are now ready to be imported into the file with Ichabod moving.

Preparing an animated character for cloth

A cloth simulation looks slightly into the future to see how the involved objects are moving. The IK solvers do not currently provide the cloth solver with all the information that it needs. This means that animation for a character must be transferred from the IK handles to the joints.

The way to do this is to *bake* the animation onto the joints.

1 Open a file

- Select **File → Open**.

- Open the file called *07.IchabodSkulk*.

  This scene has Ichabod moving from his fitting pose into a walking pose and then follows him taking a few steps.

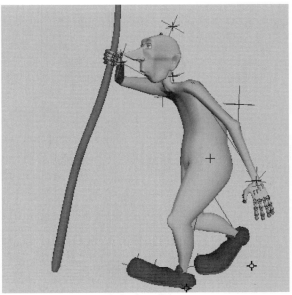

Ichabod walking

2 Bake the animation

- Select Ichabod's main skeleton node called *root*.
- Enter the following in the command line:

```
select -hi
```

This will select every joint in Ichabod's skeleton.

- Open the Bake Simulation window with **Edit → Keys → Bake Simulation -** ❑, and set the following options:

Time Range to **Time Slider**;

Disable Implicit Control to **Off**.

Make sure that the Time Slider is showing the complete range of the animation.

Disable Implicit Control tells Maya whether or not things like IK handles should still have an effect. Turning it off means that they will still affect things. It is a good idea to turn it off so that if you need to tweak the animation you still can.

- Press **Bake**.

The animation will play through entirely and set a key at every frame of the animation.

3 Disable IK

Now that the animation is baked you will want to disable the IK solvers and constraints that control Ichabod.

Remove checkmarks from the following menu items to disable them:

- **Modify → Evaluate Nodes → IK solvers**.

- **Modify → Evaluate Nodes → Constraints**.

    If at any point you want to tweak the animation by way of the IK controls you will need to enable what has just been disabled.

4 Clean up animation curves

There are a few problems with the right arm. It should move smoothly from frame 1 to 10 so that the clothing moves into shape at the start of the animation.

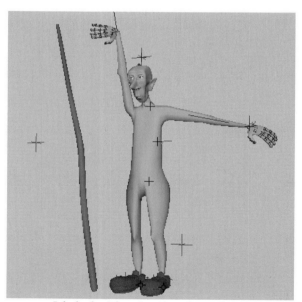

Ichabod with animation channels baked

If you look at the animation channels for the right shoulder, elbow and wrist they should jump from frame 9 to 10. The easiest way to smooth this is by deleting the keyframes from 2 to 9.

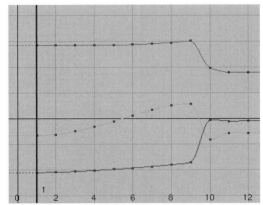

Curves need to be smoothed

- Select the right shoulder joint.
- Open the Graph Editor with **Windows** → **Animation Editors** → **Graph Editor...**
- Select the keys for frames **2** through **9** and **delete** them.

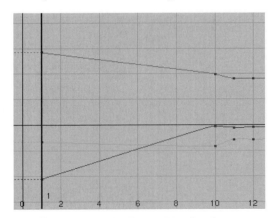

Curves smoothed by cutting keyframes

- Repeat these steps for the right elbow and wrist.

  This type of thing does not always happen when baking an animation but it is good to know how to do it in case it comes up.

  You may want to **Edit** → **Delete All by Type**→ **Static Channels** to remove any superfluous keyframes. This will greatly reduce the size of your scene file but should be done with caution as some animators like to set an initial keyframe for everything in the scene so that should they need to get back to that pose they can very easily.

A similar way of doing this is using the **Curves → Simplify Curve** tool in the Graph Editor.

Adding cloth to an animated character

Once the animation is baked onto a character, the cloth can then be added. This step will look at importing Ichabod's clothes and relaxing them onto him in his initial position.

1 Import a file

- Select **File → Import...**

  Use the default settings for the import.

- Import the file you saved in the last section called *exportedClothing*.

2 Fit the clothing

Notice that this fitting pose at frame 1 does not match the pose from the previous scene or from the previous step. You have two choices as to how to proceed: 1) Modify the clothes, or 2) Modify Ichabod. In this case it will be easier to fix Ichabod so that he is inside the clothing.

Now that the animation is baked onto the joints, all you will have to do is rotate the joints on the arms into the clothing.

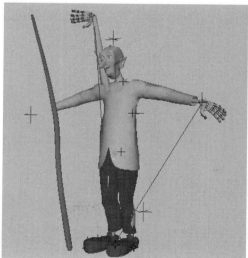

Imported clothing

- **Rotate** the joints on the shoulder, elbow and wrist to fit into the shirt.

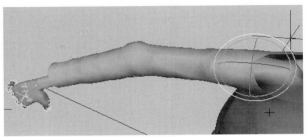

Fit Ichabod to the clothes

When doing this, try not to twist the joints too much. Their rotation values should be closer to 0 than to 360.

- Set a keyframe on the shoulder, elbow and wrist.

Note: If you have **Auto Key** turned on you will not have to set a keyframe.

3 Fit the pants

If you look at the pants you should see that the legs are penetrating through them. Rotating the legs joints could be applied here but will be a bit tricky. It will be easier to run a local simulation on the pants to fit them.

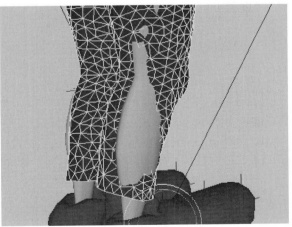

Leg penetrating the pants

- Disable the *cpSolverShirt* by selecting the shirt and using **Simulation → Disable Solver**.

- Enable the *cpSolverPants* by selecting the pants and using **Simulation → Enable Solver**.

  These last two steps can also be performed through the Attribute Editor.

- Make Ichabod a collision object with a collision offset of 0.15.

  It is important to know that if an object was ever a collision object it will have the two collision attributes. This can be misleading as the object may not be connected to a solver. You will quickly see if the object is not a collision object for the active solver so it is easy to remedy.

- Run a local simulation until the pants are no longer intersecting with the legs.

- Save the initial state of the pants in this new position.

  This may cause a problem with the pants penetrating the shirt. You can either lower the collision offset or run another local simulation for the shirt.

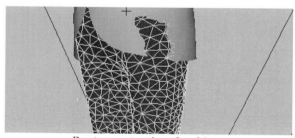

Pants penetrating the shirt

- To resimulate for the shirt you will need to:

    Disable the *cpSolverPants*;

    Enable the *cpSolverShirt*;

    Ensure that Ichabod is connected to the *cpSolverShirt* with a higher collision offset so that the shirt sits over the pants;

    Run a local simulation for the shirt; and

    Save initial state for the shirt.

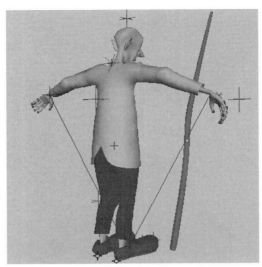

The clothing refitted to the start pose

4 Transfer the pants to the shirt solver

To run the final simulation the pants and shirt should be in the same solver.

- Select the pants.
- Select **Simulation → Transfer Garment**.

5 Run a playback simulation.

- Press the **Play** button and let the cloth solve for Ichabod's walking animation.

Make sure that the frame length on the solver is set to **0**.

You may want to specify the walking stick and/or shoes as collision objects for this simulation.

6 Compress the cache

Assuming that you are happy with the simulation, the final step would be to compress the cache. If you are not happy with the simulation you should look at the problem solving section below.

- Select **Simulation → Compress Cache**.

The cache file for a cloth simulation contains the position and velocity of every vertex in the garment connected to the solver. Compressing the cache will cut the size of it in half by removing the velocity data. This should only be done when you are satisfied with the solution as the velocity is needed to calculate additional frames in the simulation.

7 Save your work

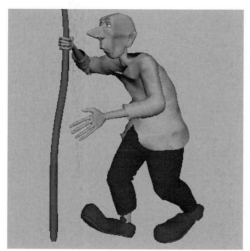

Ichabod walking with clothes

Problem solving

This section will look at some common problems that come up and some ways in which to deal with them.

Simulation is slow

Cloth simulations can be slow to solve. One of the best ways to fix this is to lower the resolution of the garments being calculated. Unfortunately this cannot always be done without introducing other problems - especially garments penetrating the character.

If you can use multiple solvers you should be able to gain some speed. With the shirt and pants that Ichabod is wearing, they could be in different solvers. This gives the added benefit of having different collision offset values so that the pants sit closer to his skin.

Another option is to solve in batch mode. This is discussed later in the *Solving in batch mode* section.

Garments penetrate the character

This can often be fixed by increasing the resolution of the garment. You may want to try building the garment a little differently so that you can increase resolution in a local area. With the shirt that Ichabod is wearing in this example, the elbow regions of the shirt have their own panels so that the resolution can be higher in this region where there is a lot of motion.

Increasing the collision offset can also help with this. If the clothing sits farther from the surface of the character there will be less chance of it penetrating.

Collision depth can lead to this type of problem as well. The cloth may penetrate with the collision object and get stuck inside. This is because the collision depth is too low and the solver does not know to search deep enough into the character to push it back out.

A similar problem can happen where the cloth gets pushed out the opposite side of the character. There is a possibility of this happening with Ichabod due to the difference in size from his torso to his wrist. The depth that works well on the torso may be too deep for the wrist and push the cloth out the wrong side. The depth should be based around the narrower areas.

Garments interpenetrate each other

There are a couple of quick things to check, should this happen:

- Are collisions turned on for the active solver?
- Are the garments in question connected to the same solver?

If the answers to these questions are yes then it could be that the resolution is too low or that the fabric is too stiff and it cannot bend to avoid penetrating.

You might also check the thickness of the associated properties to ensure that they stay far enough apart. Thickness force can also be increased to make them push apart more strongly.

Clothes fall off of the character

This may be caused by not having a collision object defined for the active solver.

It may also be caused by the character or collision object moving very quickly. If you suspect this is the problem you should increase the frame samples on the solver node. Frame samples controls how many times the cloth position is calculated per frame. The default is once. When things are moving very quickly you will usually need to have more calculations to maintain the accuracy of the solution. Increase this value in increments of one.

Cloth sizzles or pops

Sometimes you may find that the cloth sizzles or pops. It might continue to move around slightly from frame to frame when it should not. There are a number of parameters that can prevent this.

Time step size on the solver is a good place to look first. This value can be lowered in small steps (try value steps of 0.01) to try to stop the motion of the cloth.

Another place to look is the panel properties. Cloth and air damping can be increased so that cloth does not move as much.

Solving in batch mode

You can use Maya in batch mode to run cloth simulations. This means that you can use multiple machines or set up one machine to solve many scenes over a weekend.

From a unix shell, the basic syntax to do this is:

```
maya -batch -file filename -command "cpRunBatch startframe
endframe"
```

This will run through the entire simulation, save the cache file and exit Maya.

Cache Save Interval

Cloth simulation is often processing intensive and sometimes time consuming. By saving simulations in small increments this can often overcome situations where an entire simulation is lost. You can set the Cache Save Interval to any value. For example, if you set it to 10, caches will be saved every 10 frames during simulation. The default value is 0.

Conclusion

In this lesson you have looked at integrating cloth with a moving character. Bake simulation was applied to the character's skeleton so that the simulation would be calculated properly. Remember to turn Disable Implicit Control off when baking the animation in case you want to use the character's controls to tweak the animation.

The clothes are then fit to the character. Any clothes that should interact with each other are connected to the same solver along with the relevant collision objects.

When you are happy with the results of the simulation you can compress the cache file to reduce the size of it.

INDEX

Novice/New to 3D

Looking for a better understanding of 3D space and the concepts and theory behind working in Maya? Want a highly visual tour through 3D space? Try *The Art of Maya*, a full-color illustrated guide to working in 3D or get hands-on experience through one of our Maya Beginner's Guide DVDs. The Maya Beginner's Guides provide you with a step-by-step, highly visual guided learning experience to help you understand how to animate, render and create dynamic effects in Maya.

Intermediate

Transitioning to Maya from another 3D package? Looking to improve your general skills when using Maya? Choose from our Learning Maya family of books. Explore Maya through theoretical discussions, step-by-step instructions and with helpful instructor-led chapter overviews - the Learning Maya books are must-have reference materials for any Maya user. Delve deeply into *Character Rigging, Modeling, Rendering, Dynamics, MEL,* and *Maya Unlimited Features.*

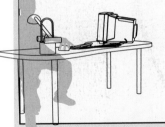

Want to Learn More?
Visit
www.alias.com/store
and check out our books and training materials.

Advanced

Are you a seasoned Maya user looking for time and money saving tips and techniques? Want to understand how your industry peers have successfully solved their production problems? Select from our extensive selection of Maya Techniques™ DVDs and learn from pros like Jason Schleifer (Weta Digital, Dreamworks/PDI); Tom Kluyskens (Weta Digital); Erick Miller (Digital Domain); Paul Thuriot (Tippett Studio) and more.

Step 1

Step 2

Step 3

Alias | LearningTools™

Maya Beginner's Guide Series

Learning Maya Series

Step 1

Foundation

Maya Unlimited Features

Rendering

Step 2

Dynamics

MEL Fundamentals

Character Rigging

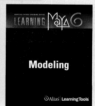
Modeling

Step 3

Maya Techniques Series

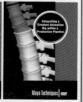